Business Recovery and Continuity in a Mega Disaster

Business Recovery and Continuity in a Mega Disaster

Cybersecurity Lessons Learned from the COVID-19 Pandemic

Ravi Das

CRC Press
Taylor & Francis Group
Boca Raton London New York

CRC Press is an imprint of the
Taylor & Francis Group, an **informa** business

AN AUERBACH BOOK

First edition published [2022]
by CRC Press
6000 Broken Sound Parkway NW, Suite 300, Boca Raton, FL 33487-2742

and by CRC Press
4 Park Square, Milton Park, Abingdon, Oxon, OX14 4RN

© 2022 Taylor & Francis Group, LLC

CRC Press is an imprint of Taylor & Francis Group, LLC

ISBN: 978-1-032-24532-4 (hbk)
ISBN: 978-0-367-68573-7 (pbk)
ISBN: 978-1-003-27914-3 (ebk)

DOI: 10.1201/9781003279143

Typeset in Garamond
by SPi Technologies India Pvt Ltd (Straive)

This book is dedicated to my
Lord and Savior, Jesus Christ.

It is also dedicated in loving memory to
Dr. Gopal Das and Mrs. Kunda Das.

This book is also dedicated to
Tim Auckley, Rory Maxfield,
and their respective families.

Contents

Acknowledgments

I would like to thank John Wyzalek, my editor, for his help and guidance in the preparation of this book.

Author

Ravi Das is a business development specialist for The AST Cybersecurity Group, Inc., a leading cybersecurity content firm located in the Greater Chicago area, and Technosoft Cyber, LLC, a consultancy devoted to offering cybersecurity services to the small- and medium-sized business sector. Ravi holds a Master of Science in Agribusiness Economics (Thesis in International Trade), and Master of Business Administration in Management Information Systems.

He has authored eight books, with one more upcoming on how to create and launch a cybersecurity consultancy.

Chapter 1

Introduction

Introduction

Back in December 2019, the mention of COVID-19 first started to erupt in the news headlines, primarily from China. There was rumor and fear that a new virus was about to plague the Chinese population, with its first outbreak in the Wuhan province.

Even to this day, there is still speculation as to how all of this started. There have been substantiated rumors that it emerged from the notoriously unhygienic meat markets or from a laboratory experiment that went completely awry.

There were even further rumors that the Wuhan University was seeking to hire a virologist to conduct high levels of sophisticated research just before the outbreak of the virus. However, wherever be the origin of the COVID-19 virus began, it was first thought that it would remain localized within China.

But as 2020 began, the spread of the virus became even more rampant in China, and also started to spread outside its borders via cruise ships that were making their respective ports of call.

Many of these passengers started to get sick, many of the ships still remain docked, and as a result, the passengers had

DOI: 10.1201/9781003279143-1

to quarantine themselves. But, there was still hope that the COVID-19 virus would still be confined to China.

But, these hopes were dashed when the virus began to make its way across international borders. Many countries in Europe and Asia started to report their first confirmed cases of COVID-19 around the beginning of January 2020.

The virus started to spread like wildfire, eventually reaching the shores of the United States. In fact, the World Health Organization (WHO) declared COVID-19 to be a pandemic in late January 2020. Because of this, the financial markets around the world incurred steep losses, especially in the United States.

The DOW and the NASDAQ displayed wild swings, going as low as 1,000+ points or more, thus triggering the financial markets to immediately stop trading until some calmness could be restored.

Although the actual number of people getting infected in the United States was still more or less mitigated, many governments at the local, state, and federal levels started to heed warnings from the other governments around the world.

Eventually, by March 2020, many states implemented shutdown orders in the sense that only those businesses that were deemed to be essential remain open.

Businesses that were not deemed to be essential remain closed for a much longer period of time, pretty much indefinitely. People were forced to remain at home and even work from home (WFH). Social distancing was mandated by staying at least six feet apart from one another. Also, face masks have to be worn when going outside. This was a rule at least in the United States for all of summer 2020. But over time, the COVID-19 virus started to ease up and the number of people getting infected started to experience a declining trend.

As a result of this, many of the stay-at-home orders were eased, and people could go out once again, and start to resume normalcy back into their lives yet once again. But no sooner that this started to occur, the COVID-19 virus started to spread again because of the closer contact among people which was allowed at that time. All of this started to take place in fall 2020, with its peak reaching closer to winter 2020.

Yet once again, people were confined to their homes and work from there as well. But by late winter 2021, and even going into spring 2021, new hopes started to emerge as vaccinations were starting to get approval from the Food and Drug Administration (FDA), with the initiation arising from pharmaceutical giants such as Pfizer, Moderna, and Johnson and Johnson. Unfortunately though, there were heavy restrictions imposed as to who gets vaccinated first.

The first group of people who were allowed to get the shot were the first responders, the elderly living in senior citizen retirement homes, and those individuals who were deemed to be at a higher risk of developing COVID-19 due to complications, such as cardiac patients or those with cancer.

But over time, more people continued to get vaccinated, and eventually, by around early summer 2021, the new Presidential Administration of Joe Biden mandated that all people, regardless of age, work occupation, or physical ailment, were eligible to receive it.

With this, many more people could get this life-saving vaccination, and because of that, the sheer numbers of confirmed COVID-19 cases drastically declined. There was firm hope that eventually COVID-19 would finally disappear and that people and businesses could return to normalcy back permanently.

For example, any venues that were canceled in summer 2020 were planned to reopen once again, and many businesses were planned to open their brick and mortar presence yet once again.

But unfortunately, as of the writing of this book, these hopes seem to be dissipating once again, with the emergence of the delta variant of the COVID-19 virus, which has literally spread all over the world. Although restrictions so far have not been so severe, many entities were requested to use face masks and provide proof of vaccinations.

Many businesses so far have been rethinking of their back-to-work orders, and these entities have extended the work from orders going into January 2021.

The bottom line is that the COVID-19 pandemic has gripped the world in ways we could never imagine. This has been truly so far a once-in-a-lifetime event, with the ramifications being far more devastating than what was thought earlier.

For example, every aspect of daily life and industry has been impacted, and because of that, people have to rethink and come up with new ways how to move their lives and businesses forward. Probably one of the greatest impacts that COVID-19 has made has been on the world of cybersecurity.

One of the largest areas in which this impact has been felt is with the dawn of the new remote workforce. Although working virtually and away from the traditional brick and mortar office is not a new concept, the way it has gripped the world has been unforeseen and even unprecedented. The concept of a near 99% remote workforce was something that was thought to happen in five or six years, more like in the middle point of this decade.

But, with the rapid spread of the COVID-19 virus, this became an utter reality in just a matter of three months. Because of the drastic quickness in the implementation of this, many cybersecurity mistakes were made which had devastating consequences.

For instance, the IT security teams across Corporate America were forced to hastily issue company devices, and not all of them had the necessary security features installed onto them. Thus, this led the American Workforce to pretty much use their own personal devices to conduct their daily job tasks.

This is a phenomenon which is literally known as "Bring Your Own Device" or BYOD for short. It posed many new cybersecurity challenges as well because many of these personal devices did not have any sort of protection. The second major problem that emerged was the meshing of the home networks and corporate-based networks.

For example, the remote workforce now had to use their home-based network in order to gain access to the shared resources that were stored on the corporate servers. Of course, there was a minimal level of protection for these home-based networks which thus exposed the corporate networks to even more cybersecurity weaknesses, gaps, and vulnerabilities.

Another strong trend that was witnessed was the drastic uptick in the usage of video conferencing tools, such as Zoom. All of the security weaknesses that were inherent in this platform were soon exposed, and the cyberattacker took full-court advantage of this fact.

A new phenomenon called "Zoombombing" erupted, in which the cyberattacker could gain complete control over any video conference meeting. Eventually, the needed soft-ware patches and upgrades were created and deployed to mitigate this from happening again, and in fact, to this day, there have been no substantial "Zoombombing" cases reported. But because of this, other video conferencing platforms started to receive greater attention, such as WebEx and Microsoft Teams.

Another key cybersecurity area that received a lot of atten-tion was the sheer and utmost importance of the creation, implementation, and deployment of much-needed incident response, disaster recovery, and business continuity plans.

Before the COVID-19 pandemic erupted, this was a key area that was completely ignored by the C-Suite in Corporate America, especially the CIO and the CISO. But with the new expectancy of the remote workforce having to work from home for a longer period of time, the CIO and the CISO have started to implement these plans so that they are now better prepared to handle any sort of long-term deployment of this nature.

Had these plans been put into place prior to the COVID-19 pandemic, perhaps many of the cybersecurity risks that were associated with deploying the remote workforce for the first time could have been greatly mitigated.

Another key cybersecurity lesson that has been learned from all of this is that the traditional virtual private network (aka VPN) was not designed to sustain a near 99% remote workforce model. Rather, it was designed to work at only 20%–25% capacity.

Because of this, the VPN has literally started to break down, with yet once again, the cyberattacker taking full-court advantage of this as well. As a result, many of the IT Security teams across Corporate America are turning serious attention to what is known as the "Next Generation Firewall/VPN", which has been designed to support and further sustain for substantial periods of time the near 99% remote workforce model.

Finally, another key cybersecurity lesson that has been learned from Corporate America is the sheer advantage of using a cloud-based infrastructure, such as Amazon Web Services (AWS) and Microsoft Azure. With these juggernauts, any business can migrate their on-premises infrastructure to the cloud. Some of the key advantages of this include creating virtual machines (VMs) and virtual desktops (VDs) so that companies will not have to hastily issue company devices like the first time around, as previously reviewed.

Second, the remote workforce can access all of the shared resources that they need in a very safe and secure manner, even using their own personal devices, without any security risks that are posed.

So far, we have provided an extensive review of the timeline of the COVID-19 virus and the cybersecurity issues it has brought along with it. Thus, the primary purpose and intention of this book is to serve as "How to Guide" in order to survive, from the standpoint of cybersecurity, the next major catastrophe to occur, whether it is another pandemic, a natural disaster, or even a human-made disaster. Although it has been written in mind primarily for the CIO or the CISO, anybody who is in a leadership role even to the slightest degree will greatly benefit by reading this book.

As a result, this book is divided into the following chapters:

- Chapter 1: The Molecular Biology of the COVID-19 Virus;
- Chapter 2: The Cybersecurity Lessons That Have Been Learned from COVID-19
- Chapter 3: How to Prepare for the Next Breed of the COVID-19 pandemic;
- Chapter 4: Conclusions

The Molecular Biology of the COVID-19 Virus

The Background

As mentioned earlier in this chapter, the first known case of the COVID-19 virus was identified in the Wuhan province of China. The first patient to be hospitalized was complaining of symptoms that were very closely related to those of pneumonia. Various types of broncho-based veloar samples were taken, and the results of the first tests that were conducted revealed something that was very close to the beta version of the COVID-19 virus.

Also, the test was further elaborated upon by further sequencing the entire genome of this new strain in order to further expose the nanopore sequencing that was to be present. Further in silico analysis based upon the concepts of bioinformatics revealed that this newly found virus was actually related to the beta version of the COVID-19 virus.

A number of in silico-based studies with samples taken from the very first patient confirmed that this new virus was very much closely aligned to the molecular genomic structure of the SARS-based COVID-19 viral strain of BatCov.

Subsequent studies revealed that the COVID-19 virus is actually a single-stranded ribonucleic acid (RNA) virus, which belongs to the SARS group of viruses. The actual COVID-19 virus is very much spherical in nature, with many small spike proteins on its surface. The genome of the virus is only 27–30 Kb, and it consists of the following protein structures:

- The membrane (M) protein (M);
- The envelope protein (E);
- The spike protein (S);
- The nucleocapsid protein (N).

It is very important to note that these above four proteins are the primary catalysts for the rapid spread of the COVID-19 virus, and the miniature spikes on the surface of the virus allow it to anchor onto the host cell membranes of the other potential carriers as it spreads.

The Key Regions Found in the Novel Corona Virus

It is important to note that the information and data that are presented in this section have come from the National Center for Biotechnology Information, also known as the "NCBI". Also, this premier database has straight and direct access to both the genetics- and protein-related information and data of many of the viral organisms that currently exist.

These data provide information of the SARS-based COVID-19 virus. The protein structures that are present in the COVID-19 virus were provided in the previous section. So far, it has been reported that the COVID-19 virus has one of the longest genomic regions in the entire NCBI database. The following are some noteworthy characteristics of the COVID-19 virus:

- The entire genome is 29,903 bp in length;
- The first 256 regions are linearly sequenced;
- There is a distinct region that lies in between the genomic regions numbered 266 and 21555;

- The S protein (as discussed in the previous section) that lies in between regions of 21,536 and 25,384 consists of a subgroup, which is technically known as the "surface glycoprotein";
- The ORF3a gene that is found within the COVID-19 virus lies in between the genomic regions 25,393 and 26,220;
- The E protein (also discussed in the previous section) is found in between the genomic regions of 26,245 and 26,372;
- The M protein (also discussed in the previous section) and its glycoprotein counterpart lie in between the genomic regions 26,523 and 27,191;
- The ORF6 gene is also found between the genomic regions of 27,202 and 27,387;
- The ORF7a gene is also found between the genomic regions of 27,394 and 27,759;
- The ORF8 gene is also found between the genomic regions of 27,984 and 28,259;
- The ORF10 gene is also found between the genomic regions of 29,5584 and 29,674;
- The N protein (also discussed in the previous section) and its phosphoprotein counterpart lie in between the genomic regions of 28.724 and 29,533;
- The final gene in the COVID-19 virus which is known as 3 prime UTR lies in between the genomic regions of 29,675 and 29,903.

After these data were collected by the respective scientists, various high-level tests were conducted which confirmed the hypothesis that the novel COVID-19 virus is indeed part of the SARS family. There have been previous outbreaks of the latter, which have been known to cause severe respiratory failures in patients affected by the virus.

The statistical correlation between the SARS viruses and the novel COVID-19 virus is as high as 100%. Also, it was concluded that the genomic regions as described above are very identical to those that are found in the SARS family. Another test was conducted to further examine the above-stated genomic regions, and further, it was discovered that there are no discrepancies between the SARS family and the novel COVID-19 virus. Once again, the statistical correlation was as high as 100%.

This simply proves that the novel COVID-19 virus simply just did not evolve on its own merit, but rather it literally grew from the SARS family. Further, the novel COVID-19 virus was also compared to the MERS corona virus (also known as "MERS") and the Bat-CoV versions of it. However, the statistical correlation that was achieved was only at 70.58%, thus revealing a rather tight closeness between these two groups.

This statistical degree of similarity is found in between the genomic regions of 13,670 and 17,861. The main protein structure is the ORF1ab polyprotein. Also, this study found that there is some statistical correlation between the novel COVID-19 virus and the Bat-CoV version, but it is not very significant. Finally, it was deemed that the ORF1ab polyprotein occupies the major portion of the genome in the novel COVID-19 virus and actually has a very strong similarity to the MERS corona virus.

This is discussed more in detail in the next section of this chapter.

The Physiochemical Characteristics of the ORF1ab Polyprotein

It should be noted that the information and data that are presented in this section of this chapter are based from a tool called "Protparam", which is available from the Expasy-based Proteomics server. The findings that are presented here are based purely upon scientific-based amino acid inputs and sequencing.

Here are some of its major characteristics:

- It consists of 7,096 amino acids;
- Its molecular weight is 794,057.79;
- The isoelectronic point is 6.32;
- The pH is 6.32, and it exists in its Zwitter ionic state;
- The total number of ***negatively based charged*** residues is based upon the mathematical summation of the glutamic acid residues and the aspartic acid residues, which is based upon 729 sub-amino acid structures;
- The total number of ***positively based charged*** residues is based upon the mathematical summation of the arginine acid residues and the lysine acid residues, which is based upon 678 sub-amino acid structures;
- The instability index of the ORF1ab polyprotein is deemed to be at 33.31, which totally supports the scientific hypothesis that it demonstrates high level of statistical based stability;
- Also, the ORF1ab polyprotein is highly water-soluble because it has a hydropathicity rating index of −0.070.

The following table demonstrates much further detail of the ORF1ab polyprotein:

Sequencing Number	Molecular Name	Molecular Length	Functionality
1	Nsp1	115aa	This is the N terminal cleavage from this polyprotein and is based upon RNA replication and processing.
2	DUF3655	68AA	This is located in the SARS version of the COVID-19 virus and consists of 70 amino acids.

(Continued)

3	A1pp	129aa	This is a submodule of the polyprotein and consists of 70 amino acids.
4	SUDM	143aa	This is used as a locator for the nonstructural protein of Nsp3. It is typically found in the SARS-based COVID-19 virus and other related polyproteins.
5	Nsp3_PL_2Pro	65aa	This is found in the bat-based version of the COVID-19 virus, and consists of 70 amino acids. It is the by-product of the Nsp3 nonprotein structure and can be associated with other polyproteins that are found in the novel COVID-19 virus.
6	Viral Protease	319aa	This is the grouping of the viral family viruses and is similar in nature to the pepsin protease and is thus required for the proteolytic processing for the polyproteins.
7	NAR	111aa	This is deemed to be about 100 residues in total length and is only located in the most extreme cases of the novel COVID-19 virus, that also involves nucleic acid binding.
8	NSP4_C	97aa	This is viewed as the C-terminal domain of the NSP4 polyprotein. This is a catalyst when the novel COVID-19 virus binds to other cells when it is transmitted to other humans.

(Continued)

9	Peptidase C_30	291aa	This is deemed a cysteine peptidase enzyme that bonds using a specialized thiol group.
10	Nsp7	83aa	This is actually associated with the viral RNA replication process. It is helical in its basic structure.
11	Nsp8	198aa	This formulates a hexameric supercomplex which looks like an empty cylindrical structure.
12	Nsp9	113aa	This is actually a single-stranded RNA polyprotein which is involved exclusively for RNA-based synthesis, RNA genome replication, and RNA binding processes.
13	NSP10	123aa	This is a nonstructural protein which is heavily in RNA-based synthesis. It is used to duplicate various types of polyproteins, where cleavage is involved with the genome replication process.
14	Corona R_pol_N	353aa	This represents the N-terminal regions of the novel COVID-19 virus. It consists mostly of RNA polymerase.
15	Viral Helicase	267aa	This kind of polyprotein consists of ATP-like binding.
16	NSP11	539aa	This kind of polyprotein encodes the NSP11 polyprotein and further generates RNA-based methyltransferase activity.

(Continued)

17	NSP13	297aa	This actually covers the NSP16 region of the novel COVID-19 virus polyproteins. It was originally called the NSP13.

Special Interest in the Region 4406–5900 of the ORF1ab Polyprotein of the Novel COVID-19 Virus

Based on the above information and data, there appears to be a very strong statistical correlation between the novel COVID-19 virus and the MERS-based corona virus, which occurs in the regions of 4406–5900. This is where partly the evolution of the COVID-19 virus takes place for both groups and is thus further discussed in the next section of this chapter. But here are some unique characteristics of this special genomic region:

■ It has a sequencing length of 1495 amino acids;
■ It has a molecular weight of 169,186.16;
■ Its isoelectrical point is at 7.31.

The Specialized Study of the Structural Component of the Genomic Region 4406–5900

As discussed in the previous section of this chapter, there is a strong statistical-based correlation between the novel COVID-19 virus and the MERS corona virus in the genomic region of 4406–5900. In fact, this specific genomic region has a very rich evolutionary history between other strains of the novel COVID-19 virus, and these are specifically corona R pol N and the viral helicase.

There is a specific tool called "SOPMA" that allows (which is available online) specific analysis of this genomic region. But, it involves one step further that a secondary confirmation is provided for all of the associations that are found in this specific genomic region; in particular, it involves the following components:

■ The helix;
■ The coil;
■ The extended strand.

Based on the tests conducted using SOPMA, here are the results of one of the secondary tests that were conducted:

Alpha Helix	Hh	567	37.93%
3^10 Helix	Gg	0	0.00%
Pi Helix	Ii	0	0.00%
Beta Bridge	Bb	0	0.00%
Extended Strand	Ee	315	21.87%
Beta Turn	Tt	99	6.62%
Bend Region	Ss	0	0.00%
Random Coil	Cc	514	34.38%
Ambiguous States	N/A	9	0.00%
Other Known States	N/A	0	0.00%

(Source: 1.).

The above results scientifically confirm the fact that the peptides found in this genomic region are very much hydrophilic in nature.

Three-Dimensional Predictions of the Genomic Region 4406–5900

The above table clearly signifies the fact that the sequencing combinations of the ORF1ab polyprotein can also be represented in terms of structure, by the specific notation of PDB ID 7btfA. In fact, the statistical correlation of this sequencing compared with the SARS corona virus 2–based RNA polymerase is 100%. This is demonstrated by the following characteristics:

- The total number of aligned sequences: 2
- #1: 7btfA
- The matrix: EBLOSUM62
- The extended penalty: 0.5
- The total length: 1517
- The identity level: 919/1517 (60.0%)
- The similarity: 919/1517 (60.6%)
- The total number of gaps: 597/1517 (39.4%)
- The total score: 4930.0

An Analysis of the Novel COVID-19 Virus and the SARS Corona Virus Spike Proteins

As mentioned earlier this chapter, the novel COVID-19 virus has miniature spikes on its surface. In this section of the chapter, we examine this in much closer detail, as well as its biological and chemical reception with the ACE2 receptor.

Through an approach making use of bioinformatics analyses, it was determined that yet once again, there is an extremely high statistical correlation between the novel COVID-19 virus and the SARS-based family of corona viruses. In terms of the evolutionary process of the spikes, it consists primarily of glycoprotein which is quite surprisingly similar to the following:

- The bat-based corona virus (at a level of 97% similarity);
- The pangolin corona virus (at a level of 90% similarity);
- The SARS corona virus (at a level of 90% similarity).

It was also discovered that the proteins found in the spike structure of the novel COVID-19 virus are very close to those found in the SARS-based corona virus. It was also discovered that in terms of its association with the ACE2 receptor, the novel COVID-19 virus consists of a total of 38 different amino acids, whereas the SARS-based corona virus consists of a total of three amino acids, providing further scientific proof for the origin of the novel COVID-19 from the SARS corona virus.

These results are presented in the tables below:

The Protein-Protein Complex (Viral Spike and ACE2)	The Change in Kilocalories per Molecule
SARS Corona Virus 2	−12.7
SARS Corona Virus	−10.3

(Source: 1.).

The above table represents the level of binding affinity with interactions specifically with the viral spikes and the ACE2 receptor.

The Protein-Protein Complex (Viral Spike and ACE2)	The Change in Kilocalories per Molecule
SARS Corona Virus 2	−12.7
SARS Corona Virus	−10.3

(Source: 1.).

The above table represents the level of interaction between the levels of protein found in the viral spikes of the novel COVID-19 virus and the SARS corona virus. As one can tell, there is no difference among these values, thus clearly demonstrating the sheer closeness of the novel COVID-19 virus and the SARS corona virus. This further proves that the latter originates from the former. Further, it has also been determined that ACE2 receptor is the host for the SARS corona virus and that once again in terms of the ACE2 receptor, there are huge similarities between the SARS corona virus and the novel COVID-19 virus.

It was also discovered that there are very important chemical interactions that take place between the amino acid residues between the novel COVID-19 virus and the SARS corona virus strains. Quite interesting enough and also which appears contradictory is that the level of binding energies between these two strains is quite low, based on the levels of protein found in the spikes that emerge from both forms of the virus.

This simply proves that there is hardly any statistical relationship between the viral spikes of the novel COVID-19 virus and the SARS corona virus, which is in sharp contrast to other pieces of scientific evidence collected that the former originates from the latter.

It was also discovered that the level of physiochemical activity in both virus strains is highly dependent upon the mutations that take place among the viral spikes. Also, a strong level of binding is found between the ACE2 receptor and any amino acid residues, which remains even if any mutations may take place.

Finally, the association between the ACE2 receptor and the level of proteins which is found in the viral spikes thus ultimately determines how quickly the novel COVID-19 virus spreads, thus increasing the infection rate. It was also determined that the ACE2 receptor which is found in the human cellular structure is the ultimate target and host site for the novel COVID-19 virus.

Determining the Chemicals for a Vaccine Based upon the Comparison Level of the RNA Polymerase of the Novel COVID-19 Virus

When the novel COVID-19 virus erupted across the world last year (as discussed in this chapter), the rush was literally to develop a suitable vaccine in order to slow down and eventually stop the rate of infections. Over the course time, and through painstaking development in the process, eventually three vaccines emerged that were subsequently approved by the FDA in the United States.

These vaccines emerged from the following pharmaceutical companies:

■ Johnson & Johnson;
■ Pfizer;
■ Moderna.

The first requires only one shot, while the last two require a double dosage injection to the patient, at a three-week interval. There were some issues which arose after the injection of the dosage of these vaccines, such as blood clotting, and patients experienced some serious side effects after the second dosage was administered.

But eventually, these issues were resolved, and because of that the infection rate at least in the United States quickly tapered off. While other variants of the novel COVID-19 virus have emerged, most of them have been mitigated to some degree or another.

But, there was a new variant that emerged, which is known as the "Delta Variant". This has been proved to be the most contagious variant thus far worldwide, especially in the United States. What is interesting to note that it is the vaccinated population is not too much affected by this novel COVID-19 virus variant, but rather, it is the unvaccinated population, which is affected.

As a result of this, the three major drug carriers as described above are now feverishly (at the time of the writing of this book) to come up with a booster vaccination to help combat and mitigate the spread of this particular variant.

In this section of the chapter, we take a closer look at some of the major chemicals that can be added as constituents to the current novel COVID-19 virus.

Chemicals

Probably the best formulation of chemicals for a novel COVID-19 virus comes from the family of derivatives that originate from the "Guanosine" family. These chemicals have been proved to be very effective in combatting the MERS corona virus earlier in the last decade (specifically in the year 2012), and thus also prove to be as effective or even more when trying to discover the appropriate mixture for the booster vaccinations.

The following tables provide details of these chemicals:

Remdesivir

Chemical Formula	Molecular Mass	Log P	H Bond Donor	H Bond Acceptor
C27H35N608P	602.6	1.9	4	<u>13</u>

Guanosine Triphosphate

Chemical Formula	Molecular Mass	Log P	H Bond Donor	H Bond Acceptor
C10H18N5O20P5	683.14	−5.7	8	<u>16</u>

Uridine Triphosphate

Chemical Formula	Molecular Mass	Log P	H Bond Donor	H Bond Acceptor
C9H15N2O15P3	484.14	−5.8	7	15

IDX-184

Chemical Formula	Molecular Mass	Log P	H Bond Donor	H Bond Acceptor
C25H35N6O9PS	626.6	−1.3	6	13

Sofosbuvir

Chemical Formula	Molecular Mass	Log P	H Bond Donor	H Bond Acceptor
C22H29FN3O9P	529.4	1.0	3	11

Ribavirin

Chemical Formula	Molecular Mass	Log P	H Bond Donor	H Bond Acceptor
C8H12N4O5	244.2	−1.8	4	7

The Results of the Docking Studies

Various scientifically based docking studies were also conducted on the above-mentioned chemicals in order to prove their effectiveness for their usage as a potential vaccine to combat the spread of the novel COVID-19 virus. The results of this study are summarized in the following table:

Sample Number	The Ligand	The Level of HEX Docking Energy
1	Remdesivir	−276.31
2	Guanine Triphosphate	−253.83
3	Uridine Triphosphate	−204.54
4	IDX-184	−297.88
5	Sofosbuvir	−235.87
6	Ribavirin	−162.23

It should be noted that the docking procedures were conducted between the above-mentioned ligands (as described in the table) and the RNA polymerase domain of the ORF1ab polyprotein. From this study, it can be concluded that all of the docking energies can be deemed to be rather favorable, but from this particular group, it is the following ligands which could prove to be useful in a booster vaccine:

- Remdesivir;
- IDX-184;
- Guanine triphosphate.

NOTE: Source for the above tables comes from Source 1.

Determining the Criterion for an Effective Booster Vaccine

Determination of the specific criterion which will make an effective vaccine, especially for the delta variant of the novel COVID-19 vaccine, can be an extremely difficult task as there are so many variables that need to be taken into consideration.

Thus, the primary objective of this chapter is to give an overview into this process, primarily focusing upon antigenic peptides on the ORF1ab polyprotein, which has been discussed in detail earlier in this chapter.

Once again, the information and data were collected from the NCBI server (also discussed in this chapter), which were also closely examined using a scientific technique called "BLAST". Another subtechnique known as the "Reverse Vaccinology Approach" was also used.

A Comparison of the ORF1ab Polyprotein against the Human Proteome

As mentioned in the previous section, the BLAST technique was used to identify and confirm the degrees of similarity of the human proteome that is associated with the novel COVID-19 virus. It was also used to statistically gauge the degree of correlation or similarity with the ORF1ab polyprotein.

Although it could not be confirmed for sure, the preliminary results of scientific studies conducted show that there is no degree of statistical correlation yet with the ORF1ab polyprotein.

But interestingly enough, the preliminary results also indicate that there is a 31% statistical degree of statistical similarity between the ORF1ab polyprotein and the cellular structure in human beings. In this sense, it is considered to be both "pathogenic and antigenic". The latter is detailed in the next section.

A Closer Examination of the Antigenic Regions

A closer examination of the antigenic regions involves the antigenic peptide prediction mechanism. The ultimate goal of this study was to further examine which of the antigenic regions in the ORF1ab polyprotein could be the catalyst to develop antibodies against the novel COVID-19 virus, in case that a human being was to be affected by it.

Some of the preliminary results have indicated thus far that there is an entire total of 311 antigenic peptides just based from within the ORF1ab polyprotein. Thus, this helps to confirm the fact that creation and usage of polypeptides is a viable source for creating booster vaccines, especially the delta variant that the world is experiencing at the time of the writing of this book.

A Review of the EMBOSS ANTIGENIC Technique and Its Results

The EMBOSS antigenic technique is used to predict which of the antigenic sites from within the ORF1ab polyprotein can be used to help create the booster vaccine. It is important to note at this time that these predictions are based on both the physiochemical properties of the amino acids that are currently present in the novel COVID-19 virus.

Further, for purposes of this particular study, a grand total of 323 polypeptides were examined, and from that, it was discovered that the polypeptide with the highest statistical score in this regard lies in between the genomic region of 5337 and 5416. Further mathematical details on this polypeptide can be seen in the following table:

Type of Amino Acid	Level of Composition
Ala (A) 3	3.8%
Arg [R] 3	3.8%
Asn (N) 3	3.8%
ASP (D) 3	3.8%
Cys (C) 10	12.5%
Gln (Q) 2	2.5%
Gly (G) 6	7.5%
Glu [E] 0	0.0%
His (H) 3	3.8%
Ile (I) 3	3.8%
Leu (L) 8	10.0%
Lys (K) 4	5.0%
Met (M) 1	1.2%
Phe (F) 3	3.8%
Pro (P) 6	7.5%
Ser (S) 7	8.8%
Thr (T) 3	3.8%
Trp (W) 0	0.0%
Tyr (Y) 5	6.2%
Val (V) 7	8.8%
Pyl (0) 0	0.0%
Sec (U) 0	0.0%

(Source: 1).

Other important characteristics of this study:

- The total number of amino acids: 80
- The molecular weight: 8764.23
- The theoretical Pl: 8.57
- The total number of negatively charged residues between Asp and Glu: 3
- The total number of positively charged residues between Arg and Lys: 7
- The isoelectric point: 8.57

It is important to note that the latter statistic is actually inactive in the presence of an electrical field. Also, the three-dimensional structure of this polypeptide was determined using the ArgusLab software. It is quite effective for the modeling and building of protein models.

Based on this study, the amino acid which has the greatest potential to be used as a booster vaccine helps combat the spread of the delta variant of the novel COVID-19 virus. The molecular energy of this particular amino acid was calculated to be 2,523.94 kcal/molecule.

Other Possible Treatments for the Novel COVID-19 Virus

While the most attention, research, and resource allocation has been dedicated to the discovery of vaccines that can be used to mitigate the spread of the novel COVID-19 virus, scientists have also turned their attention toward other potential candidates in this regard, especially those that are more homeopathic in nature. In other words, the thinking in the scientific community is that while the vaccine approach is the best one to take at the present time, it is still deemed to a rather harsh form of treatment.

The primary reason for this is that the long-term effects of these vaccines on the human physiology are not known yet with certainty. While the short-term effects are negligible, the longer ones could be proved to be far more devastating. For example, after taking the second dosage of both Moderna and Pfizer vaccines, many people have reported very uncomfortable side effects that have continued on for days.

Thus, there is school of thought that perhaps a more herbal-based approach would be far more gentle, be palatable to the human body with no harsh, long-term side effects. Potential solutions are examined in more detail in this section of the chapter.

Zingiber officinale

Simply put, *Zingiber officinale* is known as "Ginger" in layman's terms. Numerous studies have been conducted on effect of the use of fresh ginger upon the human cellular structure, in particular, in the treatment of a disease which is technically known as the Human Respiratory Syncytial Virus infection, also known as the HRSV in short. It was discovered that the use of ginger prevents the molecular binding of this virus in the respiratory tract in the human being.

Studies have also proven that just 300 micrograms will release a special chemical called the interferon beta which is highly antiviral in nature. The use of ginger has been used to combat the following forms of viruses:

■ The Surrogate Norwalk Virus;
■ The Human Respiratory Syncytial Virus;
■ Influenza.

Allium sativum

Allium sativum is commonly known as garlic. Various scientific studies have shown that this is a very effective means to combat the spread of the influenza virus. It has also been proven useful in combating other viruses such as:

■ Influenza strains A and B;
■ The *Cytomegalovirus*;
■ The rhinovirus;
■ The herpes simplex virus strains 1 and 2.

Tinospora cordifolia

Tinospora cordifolia is a typical weed that is found in grass. Scientific studies have proven its usefulness in mitigating the spread of HIV, especially when specific alkaloids are extracted and deployed.

Ocimum tenuiflorum, *Tulsi, and* Withania somnifera, *Ashwagandha*

There have been several scientific studies that have proven some effectiveness of *Ocimum tenuiflorum*, Tulsi, and *Withania somnifera*, Ashwagandha, when stopping the spread of the novel COVID-19 virus. These studies were even further substantiated by various types and kinds of in silico docking studies that the chemical composition of these various plants could stop the metabolic process of the ACE2 which is found in human cells, as discussed earlier in this chapter of the book.

It was discovered that it is specifically the phytochemicals from the Ashwagandha plant that could mitigate the chances of the receptor-binding domain (also known as the RBD) from being attached to the viral spikes that emerge from the novel COVID-19 virus.

So thus theoretically, it was concluded that the mitigation process of the novel COVID-19 virus entering into the host cells of human being was examined, which thus could greatly reduce the spreading rate of infection.

It has also been investigated if the Ayurveda herb plant could also mitigate the spread of the novel COVID-19 virus, and preliminary studies have actually proven this to be the actual case.

The Use of Plasma

The basic line of thinking in this kind of scenario is that if an individual has already been infected with the novel COVID-19 virus, then their blood plasma could be potentially used as a means to greatly the mitigate the spread of it, since new antibodies have thus been developed. As a background, the blood plasma consists of the following compositions:

■ 90% water;
■ 10% proteins from the blood stream.

It is hypothesized that the latter could very well be various kinds of antibodies, in particular, serum albumin. The separation of the actual blood plasma from the blood would be done through a process known as centrifusion. The use of blood plasma was actually first used to combat the disease of diphtheria, with actually quite successful results.

However, it should be noted that the use of blood plasma from an individual who has already been infected with the novel COVID-19 virus is no guarantee that it will provide any sort of immunity. One of the primary reasons for this is that it only works on a passive basis. In fact, the use of blood plasma in some cases could very well also increase the rate of infection of the novel COVID-19 virus.

But thus far, preliminary results have shown that the use of blood plasma could still be useful. For example, when the novel COVID-19 virus first broke out in the Wuhan province of China, ten adults were tested by using the blood plasma technique. In just a time span of seven calendar days, clinical results proved that enough antibodies were produced.

This same type of study was conducted in the United States as well. In a study that was published by the American Journal of Pathology, 25 patients were given the blood plasma from infected individuals. Nineteen of these patients developed enough antibodies to the point where they could even be discharged from the hospital.

The use of blood plasma has also proven to be quite effective for the following viral outbreaks:

■ The SARS Pandemic in 2003;
■ The H1N1 Influenza in 2009;
■ The Ebola Pandemic in 2015.

But in the case of the novel COVID-19 virus, it is important to note that in order to yield the maximum benefit of blood plasma, blood must be transfused to the patient within a 28-day time span after the human donor has been infected. Also, those individuals who display asymptomatic conditions are not good candidates for the transfusion of blood plasma. For some reasons, this is especially the case for those individuals that do not display a level of high fever.

The Development of Testing Kits

Apart from mitigating the spread of the novel COVID-19 virus, the other crucial aspect is the need for testing kits in order to confirm if an individual does indeed have this by testing positive for it. So far, the most comprehensive and most reliable test is known specifically as the "Gold Standard".

This testing method involves pure extraction of both the RNA composition of the novel COVID-19 virus. Then this specific sample is amplified by using various priming techniques in order to truly determine if an individual in question has it. But, the collection and interpretation of these results require a very high level of expertise and thus, can take quite a bit of turnaround time.

Another testing kit that has been widely accepted is the novel COVID-19 RT-PCR test kit, and it has also received worldwide approval for Accelerated Emergency Use, as these unprecedented times have called for this type of action. In order to carry this out, the nucleic acids are collected and examined from the individual in question.

It is important to note that this testing kit also makes use of three different primers which is injected into the nucleocapsid N gene (which was also reviewed in detail earlier in this chapter). More details are as follows:

- The isolation of the genomic RNA sequence from the novel COVID-19 virus;
- The purification of the above by making usage of what is known as the Applied Biosystems QuantStudio7 Flex (also known as the QS7) in order to further amplify the RNA sample that was collected;
- The probe of the testing kit then binds itself to a genomic region of the RNA sample;
- The Taq polymerase enzyme which is found in the collected RNA sample is then used to eliminate any extra material that may have been inadvertently collected by the probe;
- The last step in this process is the generation of a fluorescent-based signal to see if there are even the minutest of strains of the novel COVID-19 virus of the individual in question.

Other key points to be noted here include the following:

1. In order to mitigate any statistical errors from being present, a negative control has also been implemented

into the above-mentioned testing kit. It contains of a molecular-based free water sample.
2. An actual sample of the novel COVID-19 virus is also contained in the testing kit that contains the N1, N2, and N3 versions of RNA sequencing.
3. An extraction control is also used, which is the Hs_ RPP30, which further examines the collected sample for the presence of any sort of nucleic acids.
4. A negative extraction control (also known as an NE) is used for further confirmation of the presence of the novel COVID-19 virus of the individual in question.

The following are the reagents that are used in this particular testing kit:

■ The Novel COVID-19 N1-F Primer;
■ The Novel COVID-19 N1-R Primer;
■ The Novel COVID-19 N1-P Probe;
■ The Novel COVID-19 N2-F Primer;
■ The Novel COVID-19 N2-R Primer;
■ The Novel COVID-19 N2-P Probe;
■ The Novel COVID-19 N3-P Primer;
■ The Novel COVID-19 N3-R Primer;
■ The Novel COVID-19 N3-P Probe;
■ The RP-F Primer;
■ The RP-R Primer;
■ The RP-P Probe;
■ The Novel COVID-19 N Positive Control;
■ The Hs RPP30 Internal Extraction Control.

However, it is interesting to note that the RT-PCR testing is of course used in different countries around the world, but they all have different target regions for testing the presence of the novel COVID-19 virus, which is demonstrated in the following table:

Country	Health Institute	The Gene Targets
China	The China CDC	ORF1ab and nucleoprotein (N)
Germany	The Charite	RdRP, E, N
Hong Kong	The HKU	ORF1b-nsp14, N
Japan	The NIID	Pancorona and other targets, and the viral spike protein
Thailand	The National Institute of Health	N
United States	The CDC	Three subtargets in the N Gene
France	The Pasteur Institute	Two subtargets in the RdRP

(Source: 1.).

Finally, it should be noted that rapid testing kits have been developed from the RT-PCR testing kits. This allows rapid confirmation or denial of the presence of the novel COVID-19 virus of the individual in question. These tests are based on the following:

■ The lateral flow of the immune-based chromatography assay;
■ The targeted antibodies of the immunoglobulin, M-IgM and G-IgG.

These antibodies are collected from either the blood-based or plasma sample of the individual in question. But the results of these are often questionable in nature because of the number of high false positives that could emerge.

Therefore, the governments of the countries described in the last table highly recommend the use of the RT-PCR because of its comprehensive nature.

Reference

1. Amit Kumar, Ajit Kumar Saxena, Gwo Guin Lee, Amita Kashyap and G. Jyothsna. The Novel Coronavirus 2019. In *Silico Design and Drug Discovery*. Berlin, Germany, Springer, 2020.

Chapter 2

The Cyber Lessons That Have Been Learned from COVID-19

When the COVID-19 pandemic reached the United States, there were many things that Corporate America was simply not ready for. Of course, at the same time, nobody expected that something like this would ever happen. Truly, this has been a once-in-a-lifetime event, which hopefully will never happen again. But, hopefully, nothing like this will ever happen again. There are numerous key lessons that have been learned, and they are as follows:

- The macro lessons that have been learned by the CISO and their IT security team;
- The slow internet speed that resulted from the near 99% workforce (this was primarily caused by the intermeshing of both the home-based and corporate-based networks;
- The shortage of a cyber-based security workforce;
- The poor performances of the virtual private networks (also known as a VPN);
- The lack of understanding of cybersecurity risk;

DOI: 10.1201/9781003279143-2

- The lack of understanding of cyber resiliency;
- The lack of vetting for third-party suppliers and vendors;
- The lack of controls surrounding data privacy, especially as it relates to the personally identifiable information datasets (also known as "PII");
- The intermingling of home and corporate networks;
- The lack of keeping your IT security team motivated;
- The lack of a secure remote workforce;
- The lack of security awareness training programs for employees;
- Just how dangerous the dark web can really be;
- The emergence of supply chain attacks – solar winds.

First, let us get started with the macro issues that have been learned thus far.

The Macro Issues

Back in December 2019, the word "Coronavirus" was just starting to make the news headlines. Supposedly, the first outbreaks of it happened in the Wuhan province of China. But some five months later, nobody could have ever predicted the havoc that this virus would occur worldwide, especially in the United States.

Lives in the United States have been literally turned upside down, especially when it comes to remote cybersecurity risk. In this section, we examine this in more detail.

The Impacts

What are some of the areas that COVID-19 has made its mark on? Here is a sampling:

1. <u>Work from home (WFH):</u> Yes, the concept of a distributed workforce is not new; businesses have been doing

this for years. But the way in which it has happened globally, nobody ever expected. For example, the thinking of many cybersecurity professionals was that the concept of a 99% remote workforce for any organization would not happen until at least 2024 or 2025. But within the short time span of just one month, it is now a reality. So perhaps the good news out of all this is that WFH is now possible. But there was a huge price to pay. The IT departments of many businesses, large or small, had to literally scramble at the last minute to provide remote workforce technologies and other types of wireless devices for their employees. In this mayhem, many of these devices were poorly prepared in terms of applying the needed security protocols to them. Despite this, there are many employees that are still using their own personal devices in order to conduct their daily job tasks, also known as "Bring Your Own Device" or "BYOD". Because of this, there are many backdoors that have been left wide open for the cyberattacker to enter into and deploy their malicious payloads. Further compounding this issue is that the IT security teams have not been able to deploy and install the needed software patches and upgrades to these systems, as employees are using their own, private networks to login and gain access to the shared resources. Also, companies have not been able to conduct effective security awareness training seminars in order to maintain a level of "cyber hygiene" among their employees.

2. <u>Video conferencing takes a "Zoom"ing upward trend</u>: For the most part, businesses have used some sort of video conferencing tool in order to hold meetings, especially if they have remote workers dispersed in different geographic areas. But the use and quick adoption of this mechanism has been completely unprecedented with the advent of COVID-19. As a result, a majority of these video conferencing platforms have now become the

major breach point for the cyberattacker, especially using Zoom. It has become so bad that there is a new jargon that is associated with it, which is called "Zoombombing". This is when " ... meetings are being taken over by outside actors who often project racist or otherwise hateful imagery onscreen or spew abuse to users in the video chat. Worse, these hijackers are targeting communities like schools and universities, organizing efforts, and Alcoholics Anonymous". (Source: 1). Based on this definition, it is not just Corporate America that is being impacted. It is also the nonprofit sector, and even the academic institutions, all the way from grade school to universities, that are being impacted.

3. Phishing emails: Phishing is probably one of the oldest threat variants to ever exist. Its first known origins go back to the early 1990s, but the first public attack did not occur until the mid-90s, when America Online, who was the largest internet service provider (ISP) at that time, was impacted. Since then, phishing attacks have grown exponentially both in terms of sophistication and stealthiness. But worst of all, many new threat variants have emerged from this, especially ransomware and Business Email Compromise (BEC). Up to now, cyberattackers have been using primarily phishing-based emails to lure unsuspecting victims to give up their personal identifiable information (PII) on the financial websites that they use, such as banking, financial trading, etc. But with the COVID-19, this has escalated to an even greater scale. For example, the cyberattacker is now launching spoofed websites that look so authentic that is almost impossible to tell what is fake anymore. Also, they are not targeting the financial industry as much. Instead, with the fear and mayhem that has been brought up during this pandemic, they are now heavily targeting any entity that has anything to do with health issues. A prime example of this is the website of the World Health

Organization (WHO). When COVID-19 first hit, there were many spoofed websites, tricking people to download malicious documents that were supposedly educational in nature about the virus. Even scarier is that while phishing emails are still being used, the cyberattacker is now resorting to other covert techniques such as Social Engineering, "Smishing" (these are phishing-based SMS messages), and robocalls.

4. <u>E-Skimming</u>: Credit card fraud has always been an issue, no matter if you shop at a brick-and-mortar store or even online. But with COVID-19, this kind of attack has also seen a huge uptick. In this situation, it is not malware that is being deployed at the point of sale (POS) terminals in order to capture your credit card information. Instead, the cyberattacker is going after the vulnerabilities and weaknesses that are found in the source code that is used to create an online store. For example, software development teams are often under great pressure to deliver Web-based applications under budget and on time to the client. Because of this, checking the security of the source code modules becomes a forgotten about item. As a result, many unintentional backdoors are left behind. Also, application programming interfaces (APIs) are being used, especially open-sourced ones, in order to help speed of the Software Development Life Cycle (SDLC) of the project. These are also untested. Because of this, the cyberattacker now has many great avenues in order to make their grand entrance to deploy their malware which will covertly capture your credit card data, thus making information security an even greater risk. So while you may be thinking that you are shopping virtually in a safe environment, there are chances that you could become a victim of credit card fraud, even though your payment transaction appears to have been processed successfully and you got a receipt for it.

5. Domain Heisting: Ever since COVID-19 emerged in the United States in March 2020, there were at least 1,767 domains registered on a daily basis with some combinations of the keywords of "COVID", "COVID19", "COVID 19", "COVID-19", and "Coronavirus" in them. So far, there are in total well over 1.2 million domains like these that have been registered. The intent of these domains is once again to create spoofed websites offering the victim illegitimate vaccines, false information, etc., in order to lure in their PII to launch identity theft attacks at a subsequent time, when the victim will never even suspect. And when they do, it will be very often too late to do really anything about it. But the good news here is that some of the largest domain registrars have taken great proactive steps in halting the automatic registrations of these domains and cracking down on those malicious websites for which these domains are used as well in order to help protect the customer privacy of Americans. Worst yet, a majority of these domains have been hosted on very well-established cloud-based platforms such as Amazon Web Services (AWS, at 79.2%), Azure (at 5.3%), and Google Cloud (at 24.6%).

(Source: 2)

The Slow Internet Speed

Let's face it, the remote workforce is now a reality. The amazing thing is that this has been launched in just a matter of three months, rather than the three to four years many cybersecurity experts predicted it would take. But given the unexpected uptick in the COVID-19 positivity rate, the remote workforce will likely become, more or less, a permanent scene that is already starting to precipitate. There have also been cybersecurity issues involved with this; some have been worked out, while some need more smoothing out.

One such example of this is the impact on the spike of Internet usage, causing connections to be much slower than normal. According to a recent survey that was conducted by WhistleOut:

■ 35% of the respondents claimed that a weak Internet connection prevented them from conducting their daily job tasks at some point in time in the last few months;
■ 65% of the video conferencing calls (primarily that of Zoom) have either been cut, dropped, or even completely frozen while in process, because of a strained Internet;
■ 43% of the respondents said that they have had to use their mobile hotspot to supplement their existing Internet connection;
■ 83% of them claimed that it is impossible to do even half a day's work with a slower than normal Internet speed.

(Source: 3.)

What can be done to resolve this escalating issue? Obviously putting in fiber optic cabling on a global basis will take quite a bit of time to do. Thankfully, there are some other fixes that you can implement in the meantime.

How to Make the Most of Your Current Bandwidth

Here are some quick tips:

1. Consider boosting your Internet signal: This just takes some simple tweaking in your home router to boost your signal. For example, you should consider relocating your router to a more central point within your home. By doing this, the signals will be much stronger in nearly all cases. Preferably, you should avoid walls and other such barriers. Instead, try to position your router so that it is

near an open space, such as a window, or a patio door. Also, to juice up the Internet speed even further, you should probably get what is known as a Wi-Fi Repeater, also known as a Wi-Fi_33 Extender. This device will simply amplify your existing Internet connection strength.

2. Test your Internet speed: There are a number of free tools that will allow you to test to see just how quick your Internet speed is. If you discover that your Internet speed is actually slow, then your home network could very well be what most call "saturated". This happens when all the members of your family are attempting to connect to the Internet at once and using resources that are literally hogging up your bandwidth levels. For example, this typically happens when you are trying to steam an Internet video, which takes up a lot of processing power. A quick tip here is to try and limit this kind of activity until after work hours. But saturation can also exist from your ISP. If you are on a lower-tiered plan, there is a good chance that your Internet speed will be throttled down, in order to accommodate the other ISP customers that are trying to access the Internet as well. The only fix to this is to upgrade your plan to a higher tiered option.

3. Change your work hours: As we all know, traditional brick-and-mortar locations are available from 8 AM to 5 PM. But with working virtually, all of that can change. For example, the peak levels of Internet usage are typically in the morning hours, usually from 8 AM to 11 AM. Perhaps, with approval from your manager, you could start your workday at 12 PM or so, after most video meetings have already taken place. Or perhaps you could even work later hours in the night, or work on the weekends also, when the levels of Internet usage are lower. This is especially true during the summertime when people spend a lot more time outside.

4. <u>Set clear and distinct boundaries for non-work Internet usage</u>: It's not just parents that are working at home, but many kids are also learning virtually from home. But school hours vary, and with that in mind, you need to keep your children occupied with other non-Internet activities that will conserve bandwidth while you are working remotely. As previously mentioned, Internet-based entertainment can consume a lot of your band-width. Therefore, restrict this to after work time and for just for a few hours only.

The Lack of a Cybersecurity Workforce

A huge cyber problem that is compounding Corporate America is the lack of a solid cybersecurity workforce. While there are skilled workers out there, it is simply not enough today. IT security teams are now being stretched well beyond their breaking points, and the burnout rate has probably reached its highest level than ever before.

What can be done to resolve this problem? This is the focal point of this subsection.

What Is the Solution???

1. <u>Hire the young college graduates</u>: At least here in Corporate America, the trend is to hire only seasoned cybersecurity professionals. The primary reason for this is that companies want only individuals with deep levels of experience to protect their digital assets. To a certain degree, this is understandable. But keep in mind, this is a double-edged sword. For example, if only the seasoned professionals are entrusted to safeguard the crown jewels of a business, you will still experience a lack of good workers. The reason for this is that if you only want the "best of the best", you are going to have to offer a very

lucrative compensation and benefits package. This of course can take a hit on the bottom line, especially during rough times like the COVID-19. Because of this, your seasoned and most entrusted workers will burn out very quickly, quit, look for another job, or even start their own business. In the end, there is nothing to be gained. So, you have to take that chance and hire much younger workers who will most likely be fresh out of college or some kind of cert program. In this regard, it is important to think about the long-term effects. If you do hire a college graduate and train them to protect your mission critical information and data, the chances are greater that they will feel a stronger sense of loyalty, and perhaps even be your employee for a very long time.

2. Hire outsourced talent: With the gig economy now in almost full swing, there are many cybersecurity workers that are available on a contract basis. A typical example of this is the "vCISO". This is where you hire an experienced, third-party individual to literally be your CISO for a fixed-term contract. The primary benefit of this is that you do not have to pay an exorbitant salary or benefits package; you just pay a flat fee, which is typically around a few thousand dollars. These individuals will offer candid, neutral, and unbiased advice as to how your company needs to better fortify their lines of defenses. More than likely, they will also have other contacts that help to further augment your existing IT security staff, especially in the way of conducting penetration testing and threat hunting exercises, and providing security training for your other non-IT employees. Although it would be nice to have a permanent, full-time staff that you can always count on, hiring contractors is also a great way to go, especially if you do not have the budget to do this. For example, with outsourced employees, you can quickly ramp up or ramp down your staffing needs, especially if you are an small to Medium Sized Business.

But there is one especially important thing to keep in mind: If you are looking at hiring contractors, you have to make sure that they are as fully vetted as possible. There are two reasons for this: 1) You are entrusting them to the databases of where the PII of your customers are stored; and 2) If one of these contractors makes a mistake which leads up to a security breach, they will not be liable for it, you will be.

3. <u>Make use of automated tools</u>: One of the other factors that are stretching IT security teams to their limits is that on a daily basis, they are being bombarded with tons of alerts and warning messages from all of the security tools/technologies that they have deployed. At the present time, most businesses in Corporate America have to triage all of these items on a manual basis, which can take hours, if not days. Because of this, those alerts/warnings that are legitimate very often fall through the cracks, thus exposing the business to an even greater risk of becoming a victim of a large-scale cyberattack. In this regard, you should seriously consider making use of artificial intelligence (AI), especially in the way of neural networks. With this, you can quickly and seamlessly automate this process because they can filter for and discard the false positives, and only presenting those alerts/warnings which appear to be legitimate. Keep in mind that AI-based solutions are actually very affordable these days, many of them come as hosted offerings via the cloud. In turn, this makes deploying them is pretty easy. But best of all, they are also scalable, to fit your needs. The bottom line is that your existing IT security employees will not be so overburdened, and thus, will be on their A-game when it comes to protecting your business.

4. <u>Consider hiring those cyberattackers who have turned over to the "Good Side"</u>: Yes, it is quite possible like in the Return Of The Jedi with Darth Vader, that cyberattackers can turn over a leaf, and become what are

known as "Ethical Hackers". In this instance, they are often hired for bug bounty programs that are offered by some of the largest IT companies, including the likes of Oracle, Microsoft, Apple, Google, etc. They are called upon to break the new applications that these companies offer to discover any unknown vulnerabilities, gaps, weaknesses, backdoors, etc. In return, if something is found and a solution is offered to fix it, they are paid a huge bonus, very often ranging payouts in the five or even six figures. As a result, you should look into hiring these kinds of individuals. After all, you want employees that think exactly like a cyberattacker, so why not hire people who have actually done it? To do this, you can reach out to these bigger companies, and advertise any open cyber-related positions that you may have. Or, if you have some extra money on hand, you could also perhaps even deploy your own bug bounty program, and if you are impressed enough with the ethical hacker, then you should probably hire them on board.

5. Start to create internships and/or apprenticeship programs: Remember, it is especially important to spark a deep level in cybersecurity when individuals are at an incredibly young age, especially when they are in their teens, especially if they are in junior high or high school. For example, you can partner up with your local college, university, and/or even high school and offer various sorts of internships, summer camps, etc., to prospective students. If some of them turn out to exceed your expectations, perhaps you can even be a mentor to them as they enter college, and continue working with them so that you can even hire him or her as an employee for your company after they graduate. One key thing you should also consider is to offer some sort of financial help in the way of training or taking the actual exam, if they are interested in obtaining a cybersecurity certification that is relevant to your company.

The Poor Performances of the Virtual Private Network

The firewall has always been a trusted tool to use. But given just how much network bandwidth is being consumed these days, even this is starting to show its cracks to larger degrees. Thus, people are now turning their attention to what is known as the next-generation firewall (NGFW) which is the focal point of this subsection.

The Inherent Weaknesses of the Firewall

There are a number of key security issues that are inherent with the traditional firewall, which are as follows:

1. Slow network performance: While the firewall has been primarily designed to allow for an end user to log in securely from just about any remote connection, the gravity of the number of people trying to use this mechanism all at once has greatly slowed down the flow of network communications from the point of origination to the point of destination, and vice versa. For example, most firewalls have been designed and implemented in such a way that they can only handle about 20%–30% of the workforce working remotely, not 100% of them. Also, because firewalls have been so widely trusted before the advent of the pandemic, many businesses across Corporate America have also disregarded the importance of setting up baseline metrics in order to determine if their firewall infrastructure is indeed working up to optimal standards in today's environment. Because of the surge of remote employees on a global basis, there is an increasing trend with the total number of dropped connections that are taking place. When this happens, there is usually a "kill-switch" feature, in which the firewall

connection is automatically disconnected. When this happens and the remote employee is unaware of it, he or she is no longer online anonymously. Their IP address is immediately exposed to the public Internet.

2. <u>Companies may not be using enterprise-grade firewall software</u>: Many businesses, especially the SMBs, may not even have been using any sort of firewall before the pandemic hit. But in a rush to secure these connections as their employees started to work from home, many business owners probably purchased a rather cheap firewall software package from an ISP. At this point, keep in mind that the connection from the firewall to the corporate servers is not one straight, linear shot. Rather, they are many nodes in between in which the connections may traverse through before they reach their final destination. Some of these nodes could even exist in other countries where the data and privacy laws are not so stringent as they are in the United States. As a result, depending upon where the ISP is making use of these specific nodes, the firewall package that has been purchased could very well be prone to data leakage and an interception from malicious third parties during the time the network connection was established and being used until the remote employee has logged off from his or her session.

3. <u>The intermingling with the home network</u>: With the remote work environment becoming a permanent reality now because of COVD19, many home-based routers are now being used to actually connect to the firewall interface. While the home network may be secure to some degree or another, this kind of connection brings along with its own set of security vulnerabilities. For example, if there are any malicious payloads that have been unknowingly downloaded, these can also reach the servers of the business, as the flow of network communications is being transmitted back and forth. Even worse,

this kind of connection can even become permanent in nature, which is technically known as a site-to-site firewall. In other words, whatever kinds of digital goods you have downloaded onto your home network will also have an equal, if not greater, access to the network infrastructure of the business. This will only further enhance the risk level of the PII records of customers even more to possible third-party interception. Also, many remote employees are using their own personal computers or wireless devices in order to conduct their everyday job functions. As a result, there could be compatibility issues with the firewall that is being used, thus increasing the attack surface even more.

The Next-Generation Firewall

Many cybersecurity professionals agree that the age of the traditional firewall could be seeing its last days in just a matter of a rather short-time period since the trend of WFH now seems to be an exceptionally long term one. Because of this, other solutions are currently being examined, especially that of the NGFW. Here are some of the key advantages that it brings to the table:

1. It achieves full network traffic visibility: As mentioned earlier, with the co-mingling of both the home network and the business firewall, it has become much more difficult for the network administrator to actually pinpoint and diagnose any network glitches, bottlenecks, or hiccups. But with the NGFW, this should not be an issue. The primary reason for this is that it inspects each and every data packet that is being transmitted, whether they are at the various internet gateways, in the external or internal environments, or even on a cloud-based platform such as Azure or AWS.

2. Threat vectors are stopped immediately: By making use
   of advanced techniques like AI, the NGFW can stop just
   about any kind of cyberattack from happening before
   they become a true menace. For example, this includes
   previously known and newer threat vectors, as well as
   those types of highly specialized malware that can evade
   detection by antispyware and antimalware software
   packages that have been deployed at the endpoints. For
   those remote workers that are using their mobile devices
   to conduct their daily job functions, all network traffic is
   very carefully scrutinized by an automated threat detection agent.

3. Access to SaaS-based applications is tightly controlled:
   For those businesses that have deployed their entire IT
   infrastructure to the cloud, the remote employees will be
   primarily accessing applications that are SaaS based. The
   NGFW carefully monitors all access activity that is taking
   place, so that no rogue applications can be deployed
   which could potentially cause further damage.

4. The Zero Trust Framework is automatically implemented:
   With the traditional firewall, there is a certain level of
   trust with remote employees that is maintained. This is
   dependent of course on job titles/functions, as well as
   the rights and permissions that have been granted to
   every individual. But the NGFW has no level of trust like
   this, in that it requires all of the remote employees to go
   through the same layers of authentication, if not more.

5. It creates secure access points to external third parties: It
   could be the case that a business has implemented the
   use of a firewall structure, but their outside suppliers or
   other third parties that they have outsourced certain
   business functions have not. Of course, this is a grave
   security vulnerability, as it leaves the network lines of
   communications open to the entire public Internet. The
   NGFW does away with this weakness all together, by
   implementing the use of a clientless SSL protocol in

which all connections are made invisible to the external environment through a sophisticated Web-based client.

The following table summarizes the advantages that the NGFW brings to help overcome these challenges brought upon by the VPN;

Strategic Benefits	Next-Gen Firewall	Traditional Firewall
Provides for remote access	Yes	Yes
Secure connectivity is assured to some degree or another	Yes	Yes
Protects against threat vectors posed to cloud-based platforms and SaaS applications	Yes	No
Mitigates against the risk of identity theft	Yes	No
Fortifies internal networks	Yes	No
Deploys the Zero Trust Framework	Yes	No
Implements access rules and policies that permit for high levels of visibility and granular control, based upon the following characteristics: ◼ The remote employee; ◼ Type of device; ◼ Content and/or applications being accessed.	Yes	No

The Lack of Understanding of Cybersecurity Risk

One of the key items that were very often neglected by the C-Suite in Corporate America was fully understanding just what their current level of cybersecurity risk is and how it compares to their industry. Without understanding this level of risk, the appropriate controls and safeguards cannot be put into place to mitigate against the threat of future cyberattacks.

This has been a key lesson that has been learned, as well as it is not just the IT department that is ultimately responsible for this. Rather, this is a shared responsibility among the entire company.

What Exactly Is Cyber Risk?

This term can have many different meanings to both the CIO and the CISO. The primary reason for this is that calculating the level of cyber risk that your company is exposed includes both quantitative and qualitative measures. But a good technical definition of it is as follows:

> Cybersecurity risk is the probability of exposure or loss resulting from a cyberattack or data breach on your organization. A better, more encompassing definition is the potential loss or harm related to technical infrastructure, use of technology, or reputation of an organization.
>
> *(Source: 4.)*

We can break this definition down further into its two following components, as just described:

1. <u>From the quantitative perspective</u>: At this point, you and your cybersecurity team are taking an inventory of all of the assets that you have in your company, both that are digital and physical in nature. From here, based upon a numerical category system that you choose to utilize, you rank all of them from being at the highest probability of being exposed to a cybersecurity attack to those that will have the least chances of being impacted. Once you have ascertained this, then you compute from a financial

perspective, what the estimated dollar loss will be in the event of a downtime. Of course, those assets with the highest chances of being impacted will most probably have the most dollar loss associated with them. But it is essential that you quantify this as much as possible, so you will know how to fortify your cybersecurity posture further.

2. <u>From the qualitative perspective</u>: It is essential to keep in mind that if your business is hit with a cyberattack, it is not just your assets that will be exposed. You will also have to deal with the aftermath of this all, and one of the key aspects to gauge is the financial loss that will happen to your overall brand and reputation. For example, this includes perceived negativity after the security breach by the external stakeholders, the financial damage that has occurred to the brand image you have created for your products and services, as well as the potential loss of critical customers, of whom, some may never come back. Although these variables are much more psychological in nature (that is why they are deemed to be psychological in nature), it is still crucial that you try to compute a dollar loss amount for these categories, so that you can establish a proper strategy in rebuilding your image once again.

The Various Cyber Risk Models

Many well-known cybersecurity risk models are available, but the one that you choose to utilize will be primarily dependent upon your own security requirements, as well as the kinds of physical and digital assets that your organization possesses. The below is just a small sampling of the models that are currently out there:

1. <u>The STRIDE Model</u>: This is probably one of the oldest and most well-regarded models. It was developed back in 1999 by Microsoft. It analyzes those assets that you

currently have in place in both your IT and network infrastructures. It makes use of various sorts of data-flow diagrams (DFDs) to gauge the specific events that are associated with those assets, and the boundaries that they share among others.

A more detailed look at the threat column reveals what the acronym "STRIDE" means. In fact, Microsoft has implemented this framework into its overall Security Development Lifecycle (aka "SDL").

2. The PASTA model: This stands for the "Process for Attack Simulation and Threat Analysis". This model is unique in the sense that it allows you to evaluate both the quantitative and qualitative risk measures. Further, it is deemed to be an all-encompassing cybersecurity risk model in the sense that it requires input not only from the CIO and/or CISO but also from all aspects of your IT department. It also has been developed so that you can also incorporate the various threat variants that your company currently faces in its cybersecurity landscape.

3. The LINDUNN model: This stands for "Linkability, Identifiability, Nonrepudiation, Detectability, Disclosure of information, Unawareness, and Noncompliance". This model is unique in the sense that it strictly focuses just on data privacy, which is also a hot button topic these days. It makes use of data diagrams and their associated flows and processes. This stands for the "The Common Vulnerability Scoring System". This has been developed by National Institute of Science and Technology and is currently maintained by the Forum of Incident Response and Security Teams (aka "FIRST"). This is purely a quantitative-based model and even offers you various categorization schemes so that you can rank your assets appropriately. What is nice about using this framework is that you can also use a free calculator that is available at the link below:

https://nvd.nist.gov/vuln-metrics/cvss

At this moment, many people and businesses thought by now things would be more or less back to normal, but it seems like that the concept of the remote workforce will now be here to stay for a long time to come yet. But despite all of this, there is some good that has come out of this. That is, Corporate America is now understanding the need to embrace what is known as cyber risk on a much more serious level, and the gravity of trying to mitigate it as much as possible.

This is the focal point of this subsection.

How to Share Cyber Risk in Your Company

Now that you have a firmer idea as to what cyber risk is, there is yet another misconception that needs to be cleared up. It is often thought of and assumed that the IT department should bear the brunt of containing it, after all, it is their job, right? Well, quite frankly, the answer is no. In this regard, it is each and every employee all the way from the C-Suite down to the overnight cleaning crew that is responsible for this.

In other words, this takes a new, radical way of thinking that needs to be implemented quickly. So, how does one go about doing this? Here are some important points to consider:

1. You need to convey what the true costs of cyber risk are: At the present time, the average cost to a cyberattack is now well above $1.1 million, and there is only a 37% chance that your company will be able to fully regain its brand reputation in case it has been impacted. With such high statistics, the odds are you may even have to close down operations which will of course result in job loss. These numbers need to be told to each employee in all of your departments so that they can come to grip with it, as well as understand the sheer importance of maintaining good levels of cyber hygiene in order to mitigate the risks of losing their employment in this regard.

2. <u>Distribute responsibility accordingly</u>: Employees are often considered to be the weakest link in the security chain. But they don't have to be. According to the latest Verizon Data Breach Investigations Report, 93% of all cyber-related breaches come down to phishing-related attacks. Had the employees of these organizations been given proper training, the probability of being hit in this aspect would be much lower. The sub-conscience view of this is that ok, so what if we are hit? Our cyber specialists can fix it, right? Well, the answer to this is plainly wrong. The IT security teams are so overburdened these days that they may not be able to respond quickly to cut down any further risk that has been posed by this scenario, thus increasing the chances that the cyberattacker can cause even more damage. In the training that they are being given, you need to firmly emphasize to your employees that it is squarely their responsibility to keep an eye out for phishing email, and to respond to it appropriately by either deleting it or notifying the IT security staff promptly. But of course, you need to give your employees the tools to do this and keep them updated on the latest trends in phishing variants so that they can do their part to cut down om this kind of cyber risk.

3. <u>Share information and data with all parties</u>: Even today, there tend to be lines of divisions between the IT department and the IT security team. For example, with the former, they think that their job is to primarily make sure that the IT and network infrastructure are running at optimal levels, and the latter thinks that all they need to do is simply stay ahead of the cyber threat curve. While these are their unique job functions, the truth of the matter is that the two go hand in hand with each other in order to keep your company well protected. Thus, any information/data about the cyber threat landscape should not just be kept in individual silos. It needs to be shared, to varying degrees, with all departments of your

company that should have access to it. For example, research has shown that it takes at least 60 minutes (and probably even more) for a CIO and/or CISO as well as their team to respond to a security breach. This is primarily due to the lack of the communication flows that have been deployed. This response time needs to be cut down to just a matter of minutes. But this of course can only be done if those silos of information/data are shared among one another.

4. <u>Deploy the right cybersecurity framework</u>: One of the best ways in which you share the responsibility of cyber risk throughout your entire company is to implement a good framework, and the appropriate controls that will support it. Some of the more commonly used ones are as follows:

   - The PCI DSS;
   - The ISO 27001/27002;
   - The NIST Framework for Improving Critical Infrastructure Security.

While all of these are good, there is yet another good framework that is now making its splash. This is known as the "Zero Trust Framework". In other words, you cannot trust anything in your environment. Everything and anything should be assumed to be a risk. The motto here is "Never Trust, Always Verify".

The Lack of Understanding Cyber Resiliency

A technical definition of it is as follows:

> Cyber resilience is the ability to prepare for, respond to, and recover from cyberattacks. It helps an organization protect against cyber risks, defend against, and limit the severity of attacks, and ensure its

continued survival despite an attack. Cyber resilience has emerged over the past few years because traditional cyber security measures are no longer enough to protect organizations from the spate of persistent attacks.

(Source: 5.)

An Example of Cyber Resiliency

Let us illustrate this definition with an example. Suppose that company XYZ has invested into all of the latest security technologies imaginable, but despite taking all of these safeguards, they are still hit with a large-scale cyberattack, such as that of ransomware.

Not many companies can withstand such an attack, and in most cases, they would most likely decide to go ahead and pay the money that is demanded of them so that they can resume mission critical operations ASAP.

But company ZYX decided not to go this route. They refused to pay the hacking group in question because they realized that if they did pay up, there is no guarantee that they will be impacted again by the same cyberattacker, but asking for more money the second time around. In this regard, company XYZ played their cards right because they maintained a very proactive mindset.

With this, they created backups on a daily basis, and they also made use of a cloud-based infrastructure to host their entire IT and network infrastructure. Because of this, they were able to basically kill any of the virtual machines and the virtual desktops that were impacted by the ransomware, and within just a few hours, they were able to build new ones again, and transfer all information and data to them from the backups.

So, within just a day or so, company XYZ was backed up on their feet running again, as if nothing had ever occurred. As it is legally required, the CISO of this company contacted all of the necessary law enforcement officials, notified key stakeholders of what had happened (especially their customers), and immediately launched a forensic investigation to determine what had exactly happened. The next mandate was to update all of the relevant security policies in order to reflect the lessons that have been learned from this incident.

How the Definition of Cyber Resiliency Was Met

So as our illustration points out, company XYZ met all of the components of cyber resiliency because

- They were able to greatly limit the impacts of the ransomware attack;
- They were able to ensure its survival in just a matter of a day or two;
- They are now prepared to mitigate the risk of the same threat vector (or for that matter, any of its variants) from happening again.

So, cyber resiliency simply does not refer to how a business can just operate at ***baseline levels*** after being impacted. Rather, it refers to the fact as to how a business can resume operations back up to a ***100%, normal speed*** in the shortest time that is possible, and reduce the chances of becoming a victim again.

What Is the Difference between Cyber Resiliency & Cyber Security?

There is often a great deal of confusion between the two, so here are the key differences:

Cyber security refers to the tools that are used to protect both digital and physical assets. So in the case of company XYZ, this would include the routers, firewalls, network intrusion devices, proximity readers, key FOBS, etc., to protect the Intellectual Property (IP), the databases that contain the PII of both employees and customers, shared resources that are stored on the corporate servers, access to the secure rooms which contain actual client files, etc.

Cyber resiliency refers to how well company XYZ can fully get into the mindset of a cyberattacker in order to anticipate the new tools, as well as their elements of surprise in order to prevent them from penetrating into their lines of defenses and cause long-lasting damage.

In other words, cyber security deals with the prevention of theft of information and data at just one point in time. Cyber resiliency is designed to protect the business from being permanently knocked off the grid over multiple periods of time. The former takes a pure technological approach, while the latter takes a much more psychological approach, which encompasses all facets of human behavior and culture at company XYZ.

The NIST Special Publication 800-160 Volume 2

This bulletin (aka "Cyber Resiliency Considerations for the Engineering of Trustworthy Secure Systems") details the specific controls that a business must implement in order to come to an acceptable level of cyber resiliency. This is provided in the matrix below:

The Control	Its Primary Objective
Adaptive Response	Have the ability and means to respond to a security breach in a quick and efficient manner
Analytic Monitoring	Be able to detect any anomalous or abnormal behavioral patterns quickly

(Continued)

Coordinated Projection	The need to implement multiple layers of authentication
Deception	Purposely confuse the cyberattacker with regards to the main points of entry
Diversity	Use different kinds of techniques to further minimize the level of risk
Dynamic Positioning	Increase rapid recovery by further diversifying the main nodes of network communications distribution
Dynamic Representation	The importance of understanding the inter-linkages between cyber and non-cyber resources
Non-Persistence	Keep resources only on an as needed basis
Privilege Restriction	Assign only the appropriate permissions, rights, and accesses to employees to conduct their daily job functions
Realignment	Keep changing the inter links so that a break-down in non-critical assets will not have a cascading effect to the critical assets
Redundancy	Implement multiple instances of critical assets
Segmentation	Separate the network infrastructure into different subnets
Substantiated Integrity	Determine if critical assets have been further corrupted
Unpredictability	Keep mixing up your lines of defenses so that the cyberattacker cannot plan their course of action

The Lack of Vetting of External, Third-Party Suppliers

To some degree or another, most businesses rely upon other third parties in order to carry out their necessary business functions. Depending upon what your enterprise is in, this could be simply staff augmentation or purchasing raw materials in order to manufacture the products or create the services that your customers require.

Whatever it is, the days of having an implicit level of trust are over, largely due to the impacts of the COVID-19 pandemic. Now, you have to vet your third parties just as much (or perhaps even more) as you would when hiring new employees. Another closely allied subject with this is that of vendor compliance, and is also closely reviewed in this subsection of this chapter.

The Types of Third-Party Risks

At the present time, when one hears the term "risk", the thoughts of cybersecurity threats from your third party transmitted down to your business very often come to mind. But keep in mind, there are other types of third-party risks that can be just as lethal to your business. Some of these include the following:

1. Brand risk: This is also commonly referred to as "Reputational Risk". This occurs when your third party has received any sort of negative attention, in news headlines or other forms of media outlets.
2. Process (operational) risk: This happens when a mission critical process breaks down for a period of time at the location of your third party. This can greatly impact your supply chain and put a serious cringe on product/service delivery to your customers.
3. Disaster recovery risk: In the advent that your third party experiences a massive cyberattack or other type of natural disaster, this could also have a severe impact on your own business. Thus, it is important that they not only have a solid disaster recovery (DR) plan in place, but also have a business continuity (BC) plan in order to prove their level of "Cyber Resiliency" to you (this merely refers to how quickly they can bounce back from a security breach).

4. <u>Data privacy risk</u>: This is probably one of the biggest areas of concern at the present time. For example, there are good chances that you will be sharing confidential information (especially as it relates to your customers) with your third party. Just as much as you are vigilant in protecting, you have to make sure of this with them as well. If there are any security breaches that occur with your third party which involves the loss or malicious heisting of information/data, you will be held responsible, not them. This issue has become much more prevalent with the recent passages of the CCPA and the GDPR.

5. <u>Noncompliance risk</u>: Just as much as you have to be compliant with the recent regulatory frameworks, so does the third party that you onboard. If they are not, there are good chances that they could be audited, and your business could also be dragged into it as well.

6. <u>Credit (financial) risk</u>: This kind of risk can also be of grave concern, especially during this time of lockdowns. If your third party does not have enough cash flow or reserves on hand to sustain themselves during this pandemic, you should act quickly in order to find another suitable that can deliver you need right on time, without any disruptions to your own processes.

7. <u>Geopolitical risk</u>: This typically happens when your third party is located in an entirely different country. For instance, various political events could rock your supply chain, or even Insider Attacks can damage the parts that you need in order to produce and deliver a quality product.

How to Manage Third-Party Risks

There are numerous steps that you can take to mitigate your level of risk to the third parties that you hire, which include:

■ <u>Hire a dedicated individual</u>: Being a member of the C-Suite or even the business owner, your time is obviously at a premium. Therefore, you should hire somebody whose sole job is to locate, and vet out possible third-party vendors as your company needs them. Probably one of the biggest qualifications that you should require of he or she is their ability to take a close look at the security policies and the respective level of enforcement at the third party you are looking at hiring. Also, they should be able to carefully examine just how well they protect their own confidential information/data, as this will be a reflection as to how they will treat the ones that belong to your organization.

■ Launch a very detailed due diligence process: By this, you are literally conducting a background check on the third party you are planning to hire. For example, not only should you examine their financial stability and brand reputation, but you also need to pay very careful attention as it relates to cybersecurity. For example, you need to make sure that their practices and policies mesh up to the high standards that you have set forth for your own company. Not only this, but to a certain degree, your dedicated third-party manager should be allowed to examine just how well fortified the lines of defenses are fortified at your potential third party, as it relates to their IT and network infrastructures. Keep in mind that any security breach that impacts them could hit you as well, as the cyberattacker will be on the lookout for these kinds of business relationships.

■ Create an iron clad contract: Before you actually hire a third party, you must have a contract in place that spells out in detail the responsibilities that the third party has to you, and this has to be enforceable at any time. For instance, if you suspect that there could be a lack of enforcement as it relates to internal controls, then you should have the right to inspect that and recommend a corrective course of action that should be implemented ASAP. Also, the contract should stipulate that you can conduct an audit any time that is deemed necessary in order to make sure that your third party is living up to its end of the obligations.

The Importance of Vendor Compliance Management

In today's world of commerce, there are many links that exist between companies all over the world. Probably one of the best examples are the suppliers and other external, third parties that you rely on.

For instance, if you manufacture products and distribute them to the marketplace, you will be dependent upon other entities to provide you with the raw materials, as well as others in order to ensure that what you deliver to your customers is of high caliber.

But with all these interconnections, any failure at one node can have a fast, cascading effect on other parts of your manufacturing and distribution processes. One area in which this can happen is cybersecurity and it is the focal point of this subsection.

What Is Vendor Compliance?

Simply put, it can be specifically defined as follows:

> It refers to managing all aspects of your company's and your suppliers' compliance with statutory, legal, and technical requirements. It ensures both your business and your suppliers are legally compliant, vetted, and verified to access industry-relevant trading opportunities and mitigate trading risks.

> *(Source: 6.)*

In other words, you want the third parties that you rely upon to be up to the same cybersecurity standards that you have established and maintained for your business. This includes primarily two areas:

- The protection of PII datasets;
- Compliance with the recent data privacy laws, especially those of the CCPA and the GDPR.

In most instances, you will be sharing confidential data about your customers to these vendors in order to accomplish the tasks that you have outsourced to them. You must completely ensure that all security protocols are in place (like how you have them) to protect your customers, especially when it comes from the standpoint of authentication. For example, only those individuals that must access it will have their identity confirmed across different levels.

Also, you have to make sure that these third parties are also in full compliance with the regulatory statutes as just described. The bottom line is that if any of the PII datasets that you have trusted to your third party is released either accidentally or maliciously, you will be at fault for this, not them. You will be the one facing the audits and the potential harsh financial penalties that are imposed by the data privacy laws, not them.

Therefore, you need to take the time to carefully scrutinize each vendor you consider. You must have a reliable and comprehensive vetting process in place before you decide on an external, third party that you can work with. This is where the role of having a good vendor compliance program will come into crucial play.

The Components

When it comes to cybersecurity, creating a vendor compliance program can also be referred to as the "Vendor Cyber Risk

Management Framework", or "VCRMF" for short. It should include the following:

1. Implement a well-known model: True, you can pretty much set up your own checklist in deciding what you need to look for when deciding upon a hiring a third party to work with. But if this is the first time that you are doing this, it is highly recommended that you make use of an already established template in order to fully ensure that you have all your bases covered. One such highly regarded methodology that you can make use of is known as the "NIST Cybersecurity Framework". More information about this can downloaded at this link below:

   https://www.nist.gov/cyberframework

   The models that are provided by the NIST already have a listing of standards and best practices that you start using almost immediately. They also have an established list of security controls and risk management tools that not only can you implement for your own business, but also for your hired third party. A key certification that you need to make sure that your potential third party vendor has is what is known as the "ISO 27001". If they have this designation, then you can be assured that they already have a strong set of controls and procedures in place to safeguard their own PII datasets. It simply means that if that the PII datasets that you hand over to them will be as secure as possible.

2. Making sure of compliance: As you start to craft out your VCRMF, it is absolutely critical that you have a section on it in which you check that your potential third party has achieved a full level of compliance in your specific industry. For instance, if you are a healthcare organization, not only will they be bound to the policies of the GDPR and the CCPA, but also to HIPAA. A good way to initiate this process is by making a detailed list of the

cyber-related checks and balances that you have and cross-comparing that with what the third party that you are considering hiring also has in place. If there are any gaping discrepancies, then you know it is time to move on and start looking at for new partner to work with. Also, in this vetting process, you also need to find out if they have been the subject of any audits and/or fines. If there are any, then this should also be a red flag to you.

3. It is not a one and done process: Many businesses think that once they have carefully screened and thoroughly vetted out their external third parties from the outset, then all the work is done. But this not the case at all. During the relationships you have established, the working dynamics can always change, especially from the standpoint of cybersecurity. Therefore, you need to make sure that the process you have set forth to make sure that your third parties are in the levels of compliance that you expect them to be at is an iterative one. This simply means that you have the right to execute random audits on them to make sure that the same security protocols and controls are still in place as when you first hired them. A key point to remember here is that the terms for carrying out this kind of audit should be explicitly spelled out in the contract that you sign with them, just to avoid any potential misunderstandings down the road. In fact, according to a recent study by Garner, 83% of all cybersecurity risks escalate after the contract has been signed and the work has been started.

(Source: 7.)

Also, clear lines of communications must be in place as the relationship develops with your third-party vendor. For example, if they have been hit by a cyberattack, they must notify you immediately so that you can take steps to mitigate the risks of this happening to your business.

The Lack of Understanding of Data Privacy

As we now venture into the last lap of 2021, there are many hot button topics that have come to the forefront as it relates to cybersecurity. It is expected that these will continue well in 2022 as well. One of these issues is that of data privacy.

You have probably come across this when hearing about a major security breach that has transpired, or some company is the cross hairs of an audit by government regulators.

But data privacy is a rather specific term, and it is very important to understand what it is all about, which is the focal point of this subsection.

What Is Data Privacy?

A technical definition of it as follows:

> It describes the practices which ensure that the data shared by customers is only used for its intended purpose.

> *(Source: 8.)*

In other words, suppose you are a customer of an online store, and you make frequent purchases from it. Obviously, you have to hand over what is known as PII in order to select the products that you want, and to make the final purchase. This will include items such as your contact data (such as email address, phone number, physical mailing address, etc.) as well as your financial information (in particular, your credit card number, checking account numbers, etc.).

More than likely you will probably have this stored within their databases so that it can be recalled automatically when you make subsequent purchases (this is of course will save you the time and effort from having to enter it every time). Because you have an implicit trust with your online store to keep this data safe, they also have to abide by your wishes as to how it can be used.

So in this case, your PII can only be used for making purchases, and nothing more. For instance, it cannot be sold or given away to third parties in order for them to advertise related products and services to you, nor can it be given away to a market research company for the purposes of analyzing customer buying patterns and behaviors.

The only way that your PII can be used for these other types of purposes is if you have given this online store explicit consent to submit it to others. This is what data privacy is all about, which is ensuring that your confidential data cannot be used for any other means.

Any breach of this trust is a sheer violation of the many laws and statutes that govern data privacy, such as those of the GDPR and the CCPA. If there is suspicion to believe otherwise, this online store could be the face of a time-consuming fine, and hefty financial penalties as well.

Data Privacy versus Data Security

The term data security is very often confused with and used synonymously with data privacy. However, the two have very different purposes. A good definition of data security is as follows:

> It is a set of standards and technologies that protect data from intentional or accidental destruction, modification, or disclosure.
>
> *(Source: 9.)*

So back to our example, there are protective measures that your online store must take in order to make sure that your PII is not released either intentionally or not to the outside public. It has nothing to do with the actual sharing of its external third parties. Some examples of these kinds of measures include the following:

- Making sure that only authorized personnel have access to it.
- Deploying the right authentication mechanisms in place in order to fully confirm the legitimacy of the person that is trying to access it.
- Making sure that any of the PII that is transmitted back and forth is fully encrypted, especially as it relates to credit card numbers and banking information.
- Making sure that the databases that store the PII have all of the necessary software patches and upgrades installed onto them in order to mitigate the risk of a cyberattack from occurring.
- Also making sure that other controls are put into place to prevent accidental erasure or deletion of the PII.

The Key Components of Data Privacy

As mentioned earlier, both the GDPR and the CCPA have given consumers a lot of extra power to question how their PII is being stored and handled. So if you want to make sure that the online store is following proper procedures in protecting your privacy, it must provide the following to you on their website:

1. <u>How the data is going to be used</u>: The online store (or for that matter any other business) that collects your PII must spell out in clear and understandable terms how your confidential information will be used in any circumstance. For example, if it is only going to be used for processing payments and for sending you coupons and other sort of advertisements to you directly, it must be directly stated as so. Or, if they want to collect your PII

as well for market research purposes or to give to suppliers, this also must be spelled out and the reasons shared for doing so. And it must also state that they can only do this with your written consent, either via email or postal letter.

2. The use of cookies: These are simply messages from the server that hosts the website of the online store and passes them onto your device that you are using to access it. This is used to keep track of what parts of the online store you are specifically visiting (such as the different product categories, any ads or specials that appear, etc.). The purpose of this is to streamline your future shopping experiences, and to make it appear to be more seamless. Any business that uses cookies has to explicitly state this on their website and give you the right to either accept or deny the usage of cookies.

3. The right to opt out: If the online store frequently sends you email messages about business that relates to them, they also have to give you the explicit right to opt out of any future communications, and in turn, they must also delete your email address for using it in such purposes (they will still need to retain it for other purposes, such as sending you an email to confirm the transaction of a purchase).

The Intermingling of Home and Corporate Networks

With the reality that the remote workforce is going to be around with us for the foreseeable future, there are still many cybersecurity issues that need to be resolved. For example, there is still the co-mingling of home networks with business networks, thus causing the flow of network communications to be at grave risk of malicious third-party intervention.

Then there is the VPN. This has been a warrior when it comes to the safe transmission of PII datasets across the Internet, but it, too, is showing its signs of wear and tear.

In other words, there are too many pieces to be put together when trying to resolve these issues. All of the networking tools and technologies need to come under one umbrella for ease of management, and this is where the SASE could come into play.

What Is the SASE?

It is an acronym that stands for the "Secure Access Service Edge" and is pronounced as "sassy". It was actually conceived by Gartner back in 2019, when they published a report entitled the "The Future Of Network Security In The Cloud". Essentially, this is a specific methodology which allows any type of business, large or small, to have a unified network system that will allow them to bring both networking and security functionalities under one common platform.

For example, it can incorporate both the functionalities of the WAN as well as the SD-WAN with some of the latest frameworks that soon Corporate America will be embracing, and these are as follows:

- The Next-Generation Firewall (NGFW);
- The Secure Web Gateway (SWG);
- The Zero Trust Model;
- The use of Cloud Security Brokers (CASBs).

The ultimate of goal of SASE is to bring an end-to-end protection from the wireless device all the way to the servers that are being accessed, and vice versa.

Examples of How SASE Would Be Used

It is primarily targeted toward those individuals and teams that work from a remote location and don't usually often have to come into traditional brick-and-mortar offices. With the rapid explosion of the remote workforce, it is highly anticipated that SASE will be adopted by over 40% of businesses and organizations by 2024.

(Source: 10)

But it will also prove highly beneficial to those employees that are constantly on the go, and to external third parties:

1. <u>The road warrior</u>: Take the example of Tracey. She is always traveling somewhere on an almost weekly basis. In order to further expedite her workflows so that she can get them done quickly and efficiently, Tracey decides to use the public Wi-Fi system in her hotel room. Of course, accessing, sharing, and the transmission of confidential information would be a grave security threat here. After all, there is no level of encryption that is involved here, and any of these could be quite easily hijacked by a cyberattacker. The use of SASE could potentially solve all of these issues by enforcing rules that would make sure that all of the data packets that are transmitted back and forth are actually encrypted. But not only that, it would also help to ensure that the data packets that are delivered to Tracey's wireless do not have any traces of malware in them, as she could be communicating with other clients and prospects that are external to her network connection.

2. <u>The third party</u>: Suppose that Jane is an outside contractor, trying to access sensitive documents from the corporate server. Under normal circumstances, she would have to probably use what is known as two-factor authentication (2FA) in order to have her identity completely confirmed. But even under these circumstances, trusting an external third party in this regard can still pose a very serious threat. But if SASE were to be used, it would implement the Zero Trust Framework (as stated earlier in this subsection). With this, absolutely nobody is trusted,

and any individual would have to pass through many layers of authentication (at least three of them or more) in order to have their identity confirmed beyond a reasonable doubt. By doing it this way, there is almost a 100% guarantee that Jane is who she claims to be.

The Benefits of Using SASE

The following are some of the strategic of it:

- It is highly scalable: SASE is primarily meant to be used when accessing shared resources from a cloud-based platform, such as AWS or Microsoft Azure. Because of this, you quickly and easily ramp up or down your security needs. For example, apart from the characteristics described earlier, you can also implement the following:
- Threat prevention tools;
  - Web filtering;
  - Sandboxes;
  - Multiple layers of DNS security;
  - ID theft prevention techniques;
  - Controls to help mitigate the chances of data loss, whether it is intentional or non-intentional in nature.
- Substantial cost savings: Since it is compatible with the major cloud-based providers, businesses will realize substantial savings when it comes to procurement and deployment. For example, rather than having to pay a sizeable down payment, SASE can offer fixed and monthly pricing schedules that will make it affordable to any organization.
- A reduction in complexity: Up to this point, many businesses have deployed many types of security tools and technologies, from all sorts of vendors. CIOs and CISOs are now starting to understand the ramifications of this from two different perspectives:

- It greatly increases the target surface for the cyberattacker to penetrate.
  - Many alerts and warning messages are created, which creates many false positives.

    The SASE can alleviate most of this because everything is consolidated into one primary platform, and this provides two key benefits.
  - There is a sharp reduction in the complexity with regards to the lines of defense that have been implemented. For example, the security tools will now be deployed into a much more strategic fashion. For instance, instead of having ten firewalls in a haphazard fashion, perhaps using just three of them will make much more sense if they are installed where they are needed the most.
  - Fewer tools means that there will be less false positives filtering through, which means that the IT security team will be able to triage and react to the real threats in a prompt manner.
- A coupling of security functionalities: Many of the cloud providers offer their own suite security tools, and these can also be connected with the security features of SASE seamlessly. The end result is that the business will probably have one of the most secure environments imaginable.

How to Keep Your IT Security Team Motivated

With the sheer number of COVID-19 cases now spiking up to unprecedented levels and the remote workforce now a reality for probably all of next year, the cyber threat landscape is now becoming murkier, and more difficult to predict. With this, IT security teams are now feeling extra pressure to take on more job responsibilities and are being expected to get these new responsibilities dialed in right away.

Now more than ever, these individuals need to be kept motivated at all times, in order to deliver what they humanly can. How can this be done? This is the focal point of this subsection.

How to Keep Your Team on Their A-Game

Here are some key strategies that can be deployed rather quickly and easily:

1. <u>Create an environment of trust and goodwill</u>: It is one of the very basic human needs that are to be listened to and heard. In many businesses across Corporate America today, there is a sheer lack of communications between the C-Suite, the CISO, and the IT security teams. This disconnect has become so bad that nobody even has a clear vision of who is expecting what to get accomplished. Well, now that we are living in a new norm, it is time to change this and foster a sense of open communications and assurances that your IT security team will be heard from the higher-ups. There must be a two-way flow of communications established so that they know what to expect from you, the CISO. Also, they need to have their ideas and plans heard so that at least they know that their efforts are not going to pure naught. In this regard, it is very important that you spend at least a few minutes on a regular basis with members of your team, even if it is just a phone call or a simple video conference meeting, as face-to-face dialogue is the most preferred method to do this. Just the fact knowing that they are being listened to in an honest and open format will be a prime motivator of itself. In fact, research has shown that those employees who feel that they are getting support from their higher-ups will be at least 2X more motivated than other employees.

2. <u>Don't micromanage</u>: The very last thing that your IT security team needs is to be micromanaged. They know what needs to get done, so it is very important for you, the CISO, to take a step back and let this happen. Instead of having each of your employees submit progress reports of what has happened in terms of fighting threat variants, create a chain of command. For example, break down your IT security team into different subgroups, which are captained by a team leader. They should report to this person, and in turn, they should report to you. This will get rid of the fear that the C-Suite is always watching over them, which can be a huge, constant worry, and even be detrimental to getting the job done.

3. <u>Foster an environment of career growth</u>: The very worst thing you want the members of your team is to feel stifled in their current positions. Therefore, it is very important that you show care about their professional growth. In this regard, perhaps you can sponsor them to get the training that is needed in order to pass an exam for a cybersecurity certification that they have been wanting to get. Also, try to have training sessions on a weekly basis to keep your team members current on the latest threat variants that are coming out and perhaps even provide an educational forum for them so that they can learn more about the latest security tools and technologies that can be used to combat on a real-time basis. Remember, you always want your IT security team members to maintain as much of a proactive mindset as possible. You want them to take down potential threats well before even they become a real one. Showing that you are personally vested in their respective career goals and interests will greatly help to foster that.

4. <u>Offer rewards</u>: One of the primary ways of motivating your team members is to offer some sort of

monetary-based incentive. Yes, budgets are now tight with all of the uncertainty that is currently transpiring, but even small and simple rewards will go a long way. For example, if one group from your IT security team exceeds their goals in how quickly they can react to and triage real cyber threats, you can offer to take them out for a nice dinner somewhere, or even offer gift cards in lieu of that. Also, with working from home (WFH), those employees that are working remotely most of the time obviously need to get out and do something different. With this in mind, perhaps you, the CISO, could even offer them to get substantially reduced gym memberships so that they can work out to help relieve the stress they are experiencing. But of course, if your budget allows for it, giving out cash awards is probably the best motivator of all to show your appreciation for their loyalty and dedication to their cyber jobs.

5. <u>A little can go a long way</u>: This is something that will cost you no money whatsoever: Always keep telling your IT security team about the good job that they are doing, even if something does not appear to go right. Given the sheer pressure that they are under on a daily basis, the last thing that your members want to hear is about what a poor job that they have done. This will not only break their spirit but also cause them to take "Who cares?" kind of attitude, which is something you do not want at all. Instead, if there is something that you think needs to be improved or made better, take the route of offering tactful, constructive criticism. In other words, instead of chastising them, say "Hey, maybe you could implement this instead of what is currently being done". Then follow that up with a healthy dose of positive feedback. Remember, even a little pat on the back on a daily basis can ignite human motivation to degrees that even you may not have ever seen before.

The Lack of a Secure Remote Workforce

The COVID-19 pandemic has certainly changed this world to degrees that were unexpected. Although many bad things have occurred from it, believe it or not, there are actually a few silver linings. Probably the biggest impact made has been the remote workforce. This was a concept that many experts thought would not evolve until at least three to four years down the road. Luckily for many, adjustments were made early on that allowed many to keep their jobs by simply changing their work location to their homes.

As of right now, we have seen this change happen in just a span of a couple of months. There are still issues to be worked out in this regard, but the remote workforce is nowhere to stay, probably on a permanent basis. Since this is the new norm, it is imperative that you safeguard your employees to the greatest extent possible.

The Top Ways to Ensure Cybersecurity

Here are some key takeaways to not only make sure that your remote employees maintain good levels of cyber hygiene but also that your digital assets remain safe:

1) <u>Make sure that work-related matters are done on company-issued devices</u>: In the rush to WFH in late March, many businesses across Corporate America hastily gave to their employee's company devices that did not have all the security features installed onto them. As a result, many people started to use their own devices (especially Smartphones) in order to conduct their daily job tasks. Of course, this can be a grave security concern, as these personal devices probably do not typically have the security features deployed onto them as spelled out by your security policy. But now that the remote workforce

is here to stay, you can now issue to your employees newer devices that have all these features installed on them. As you send them out, be sure to remind your employees of the security risks of using their own wireless devices and the consequences of not abiding by this policy.

2) <u>Avoid public hotspots</u>: True, your employees can only work for so long at home before the thoughts of working somewhere else, especially in public, become a strong appeal. Very few people enjoy the isolation of working totally from home. While you cannot prevent this from occurring, you need to remind them of the dangers of using public Wi-Fi at the local Starbucks or Panera Bread. For example, these types of network connections are unencrypted, meaning that any information and data transmitted back and forth from this connection is sent over as plaintext, which can be easily intercepted. Therefore, your employees must, at all times, use a secure Wi-Fi connection, such as the hotspot on their Smartphone. But in the end, should they choose to do their job in a public place, they should be making use of a VPN. This is a network protocol that creates a "masked" line of network communications. This line is invisible to the outside world. Getting a robust VPN package is actually very cheap these days and can be installed fairly quickly.

3) <u>Always make use of encryption</u>: Apart from making sure that the flow of communication is safe, you also need to deploy encryption tools on all of the devices that you issue to your remote workforce. That way, any information or data that is transmitted will be rendered into a garbled state. If that information is captured by a malicious third party, it will remain useless to them. The use of this kind of tool is an absolute must from sending out emails to even having video conferences on Zoom, WebEx, Microsoft Teams, etc.

4) <u>Deploy multifactor authentication (MFA)</u>: Typically, most organizations have made use of 2FA in which only two authentication mechanisms are used. But even this is proving to be weak, as the cyberattacker can break through this type of setup. Therefore, it is absolutely critical that you deploy MFA, in which at least three or more levels of authentication are used. This allows you to fully confirm the identity of the people that are logging into your IT and network infrastructure. Better yet, it is even better to make use of a methodology known as the Zero Trust Framework, in which absolutely nobody is trusted implicitly. As a result, each and every individual that is trying to gain access to your shared resources has to go through the same, rigorous standards in order to prove they are who they claim to be. Also, this framework instills into your business multiple lines of defenses as well, so in case the cyberattacker is able to break through one, the statistical odds of them going in further become much less.

5) <u>Implement endpoint security</u>: This is often an area that has been neglected by many businesses. The endpoints are where the lines of communication originate (such as your employee's device) to where they terminate (like the server where the shared resources are trying to be accessed). Therefore, it is equally important that you harden these endpoints, not only with the latest software patches and upgrades, but also with most up-to-date antivirus antimalware software packages available today. Also, in this regard, keep an eye out for any suspicious or anomalous behavior that might be precipitating at these endpoints. Using both AI and machine learning (ML) technologies can be a huge advantage here, as they can help automate this process while your IT security team focuses on other critical issues at hand.

6) <u>Make use of remote wiping</u>: It could also be the case that your remote employee could lose or have their device stolen if they are not careful with it. If this were to happen, over the course of time, it is quite possible that a cyberattacker could "jailbreak" into the operating system of the device, and attempt to gain root access. Therefore, once you know that the device is missing, you must issue what is known as a "Remote Wipe". This will ensure that all information and data that reside on the device is quickly eliminated.

The Lack of Security Awareness Training for Employees

Over the course of this year, and especially with the evolution of the COVID-19 pandemic, one of the most heard of topics is cybersecurity training for your employees. While this is necessary, this can actually be a hard task to accomplish.

For example, during the training, you have to keep your employees engaged and motivated to pay attention as to what they are being taught. Second, you want them to be able to foster a reasonably strong level of cyber hygiene after they have been trained.

The bottom line is that if you lose the interest of your employees in the training, then they will also be much less motivated to help you to protect your digital assets. In this subsection, we examine some of the key components of what makes an "awe-inspiring" cyber training program.

The Components

The bottom line is that in order for your employees to remember and put into motion what they have learned, it takes a combination of making the training scary, fun, exciting, competitive, etc. Here are some techniques that you can use:

1) <u>Utilize the concepts of gamification</u>: As the name implies, you make your training into a game. In other words, it's like filling in a jigsaw puzzle. You put in some of them, but then motivate your employees to put in the rest of the pieces. First, you have to introduce them to the issue of what you want to teach. For example, it could be about ransomware. In this instance, you instruct them as to how this threat variant actually takes place (no need to get into all the technicalities here – if you do so, you will lose them instantly). Then, after you have done this, you engage your employees with simulation exercises in order to garner their interest further. But to motivate them even more, you award points and recognition badges after they have successfully completed a particular task. For example, if they have successfully detected the beginnings of an attack (such as getting a phishing email), then you will award them with an honorary badge by taking the right steps to mitigate, such as deleting the email and notifying the IT security team about it. If you use gamification in your cyber training, it is important to break your employees off into teams in order to foster a more collaborative environment.

2) <u>Make the training relatable</u>: One of the best ways to make your employees understand the full ramifications of a cyberattack is to actually talk about a real-world scenario in which it actually occurred. But, in order to make its full impact, you need to discuss it in a way in which it has impacted somebody that they are close to, such as another coworker. But more importantly, it will make the strongest impression if you can bring this person in that has been impacted to directly talk about it. For example, if an employee in your company has become a victim of identity theft, perhaps you can get

that person to discuss how he or she found about it, how it affected their daily lifestyle, and the steps that they have taken to mitigate the risks and prevent this from happening again in the future.

3) <u>Make them laugh</u>: Yes, cybersecurity is a very serious thing, but you know what? Remember this old saying, laughter is one of the best forms of medicine? It is, but recent studies have also shown that laughter is also one of the best ways in order to cultivate a sense of trust and goodwill among your employees in order to make them learn (Source: 1.). One good way to make this happen is to have your employees perform in various funny skits, which simulates a real-world security breach. For instance, you can have one play the role of a cyberattacker, while the other plays the role of the administrative assistant. In this regard, you can mimic a social engineering call in which the goal is to wire a large sum of money from the company into a phony, offshore bank account.

4) <u>Introduce variety</u>: One of the very worst things that you can do in a cyber training program is to give a lecture-style format going on and on for a long period of time. This is a guaranteed way to lose the interest level of your employees just in the first ten minutes. So instead, mix up the training program by implementing a sense of variety into it. For instance, the first part can be a lecture about phishing emails, then a game, followed by a real-life story. With this kind of approach, one can almost bet that your employees will walk away after the training is over with a much better sense as to how to identify a phishing email, and the corrective steps that need to be taken after one has actually been received.

5) <u>Make videos</u>: At the end of the cyber training, one of the best ways to recap the major points is to put them all into a video, which can also add a further avenue for more variety. It is important to keep this video short, no more than four to five minutes in total length. Once again, the

video should not be about someone just talking, it should also be somewhat engaging, such as making use of cartoon-like characters in order to keep up the interest level of your employees.

The Dangers of the Dark Web

In today's world, especially given the situations that we are with both the COVID-19 pandemic and the realities of the remote workforce that is going to be with us for a long time to come, the need for the Internet has never been greater than ever before. For example, we need to access many different websites, online portals, the company intranet, and yes, even Google, in order to conduct and execute our daily job functions.

While the Internet is a gargantuan repository of such stuff (in fact, at the present time, there are some 1.7 billion websites that are currently available), this is only just a very small percentage that is out there. There is yet another huge expanse of it that exist, which many people have not even heard of yet. This part of the Internet is known as the "Dark Web" and is the focal point of this subsection of this chapter.

What Is the Dark Web?

As just noted, the Internet that is made available and that can be accessed by the public at large is technically known as the "World Wide Web", also known as "www" in the URL, or domain of the website in question. Believe it or not, this only makes up about 4% of the total Internet.

The Deep Web

The remainder comes from what is known as the "Deep Web" (at 90%), and only a small portion of that actually consists of the "Dark Web" (6%).

One of the key distinctions between the World Wide Web and the deep web is that with the former, all of the 1.7 billion websites and their corresponding are known as "Indexable". Meaning, on a 24 × 7 × 365 basis, the search engines of Google, Yahoo, Bing, AOL, etc., are constantly ranking both current and new websites based upon both the search engine optimization (SEO) and the keywords that have been implemented into their respective content.

The end result of all this is that is when you conduct a certain web-based query, only the most relevant results will be displayed instantly just within the first one or two pages of the search results. There will of course be others as well, but they will be filtered based upon their level of relevance in subsequent search page results.

But with the deep web, none of the websites and their corresponding pages are indexed. That is one of the major reasons why they are not made available to the public. However, they can still be accessed, but you need to have the special tools to do it safely, which will be addressed later in this subsection. The terms dark web and the deep web are often used interchangeably, but in reality, the two are actually very different.

As can also be seen from the above illustration, the deep web is what it can be deemed to be "neutral". In other words, it just consists of websites and resources that have been established there by other entities that do not want their material to be accessed by the public, and out of plain view. Some good examples of this include the federal government, organizations in the healthcare industry, as well as other research and development entities. There is nothing illegal in accessing this part of the Internet. Some of the other key differences between the deep web and the dark web Internet are as follows:

▪ The deep web is also known as the "Invisible Academic" for reasons just stated;

- Most of the domain extensions in the deep web are that of the ".onion" and ".12p", very much unlike the traditional ".com" domain extensions used by the public Internet;
- The data size of the deep web is currently estimated to be at 7,500 terabytes. It only consists of about 20,000 websites, but has more than 500X of information and data than what the public Internet currently possesses;
- In order to conduct transactions on the deep web, only virtual currencies are used, such as Bitcoin.

The Dark Web

Now with the dark web, this is considered to be the much more "sinister side" of the deep web. For example, this is where most of the illegal activities take place, as well as all of the criminal-based chat and messaging forums. In fact, after a cyberattacker has launched their threat vectors, all of the valuable PII datasets that are hijacked eventually make their way down here, so that they can be sold for a rather nice private, or even be used to launch subsequent cyberattacks. Other illegal activities that take place on the dark web include the following:

- It is a dumping ground for other confidential information that is stolen, which includes primarily credit card numbers and other relevant banking/financial data;
- The ability to obtain other types of payment cards, forged with stolen credit card numbers;
- How-to guides are available on how to totally extort and defraud just about any business in virtually all sorts of industries;
- The source code that is leaked from a threat variant (such as that from an SQL injection attack) often make

their way here as well. This allows for even the competition of a business to take complete advantage of this for their own nefarious purposes;

■ There are ready-made phishing templates and other illegal forms of documentation that guide the cyberattacker in launching a security breach quickly and easily;

■ Much more nefarious planning activities take place here as well, especially as it relates to human trafficking;

■ There are already prefilled tax returns with real and legitimate taxpayer information so that the cyberattacker can file fraudulent tax returns in order to get any refunds;

■ Fake passes (such as fictitious passports, driver's licenses, military-based IDs) are also available here so that a cyberattacker can launch a social engineering attack in a very sophisticated way.

There is much more that goes on; the above is only just a part of it. Now, the next question comes: "Although the dark web is the place for all the nasty and illegal stuff to happen, is still illegal to access it?". Technically know it is not. But it all comes down to what kind of activities you are doing in the dark web. Obviously, if you are engaging in some sort of criminal activity, then yes, this is obviously illegal to do. But if you are simply going down into the dark web to see what it is like, then no, this is not illegal.

In fact, many law enforcement agencies and even IT security teams across Corporate America routinely access the dark web in order to collect pieces of evidence in order to build a case for subsequent prosecution and arrests; and the latter penetrates the dark web in order to make sure that there are no hijacked PII datasets in it. If there is, then this is the first obvious sign that an organization has been covertly breached into by a cyberattacker.

How to Access the Dark Web

When we access the public portion of the Internet, it is very easy, and in fact, it is a process that we take highly for granted until we don't have an Internet connection for some reason or another. But accessing the dark web is a totally opposite scene. You simply cannot access it via any regular browser (such as that of Google Chrome, Microsoft Edge, Firefox Mozilla, the iOS Safari, etc.). Rather, you need a specialized web browser, as well as other tools in order to access it. So, here is how to do it, on a high-level basis:

1. <u>You need to download and install the TOR web browser</u>: As we discussed previously, one of the main file extensions that is supported by both the deep and dark web is that of the "onion". Therefore, you will need a web browser that can handle any sort of web requests that are made off of this extension. One such is known as the "TOR" browser. It was actually designed and created a long time ago in the US intelligence community as a means to access highly classified documents, and to engage in any form of online communications that was deemed to be highly classified in nature. It is actually a specialized version of the Firefox web browser, so the overall UI/UX environment will be pretty much the same. It also has safety features incorporated into it, so that you "surf" the dark web anonymously. In other words, it is designed so that any attempts made by other malicious third parties to find your identity cannot happen. It even provides recommendations on a real-time basis on how to stay safe as you are working your way around the dark web. You can download the TOR browser at this link:
   https://www.torproject.org/download/
2. <u>Download a highly reliable virtual private network (VPN) service</u>: While there are many ISPs out there that offer

very cheap VPN services, it is also very important to keep in mind that you go with one that is not only highly reliable but also designed specifically for accessing the dark web. One such VPN service that has both of these characteristics is known as "ExpressVPN", and it can be downloaded from this link:

https://www.expressvpn.com/

At this point, keep in mind that while the TOR browser can **mask your identity**, it cannot mask **your true physical location**. This is where ExpressVPN will come into play.

3. Be careful of the search engine that you use: While Google may be the search engine of prime choice on the public Internet, it is not available for use on the dark web. Rather, there is a safe alternative to use when it comes to this part as you surf through the dark web, and it is known as "DuckDuckGo". When using this search engine, your queries and key word searches will be hidden from view. It can be downloaded at this link:

https://duckduckgo.com/

4. You need an email address: Just like the public Internet, you also need to have an email address from which you can access stuff from the dark web. Therefore, you need an email address **that is completely untraceable, and using the ones from Yahoo and Google will simply not suffice**. TOR has a couple of email services that you can use in this regard, which are the "TORbox" and the "Mail2Tor". Keep in mind that you will need to have a TOR browser up and running before you can download any of the email services.

How the Whole Process Works

Now that you have a more solid background on what you need to access from the dark web, the next question that you may have is: "How does all of this come together?" Well, the answer to this is actually pretty simple: It is the connection which is known technically as the "TOR Over VPN".

In this kind of network activity, all of the requests that you place over your TOR browser first are sent to the VPN service that you are using, and from there, it goes through the TOR network, making at least three separate network-based hops before you reach your final destination on the dark web.

But here is one caveat. The VPN service that you are currently using to access the dark web keeps track of metadata logs. This means that any queries, keyword searches, or even any websites that you visit on the dark web are being recorded and kept track of.

The Challenges for Law Enforcement

While policing the public Internet can be a relatively complex task, this is compounded even more in the dark web, given the fact of the high level of degree of complexity that is involved. While there are many obstacles that are involved, the matrix below provides an overview of just what some of the challenges are when law enforcement officials and even digital forensics investigators face when trying to collect evidence on the dark web:

The Challenge	Why It Is So
Higher levels of encryption	There is more of this on the dark web than the public Internet. Because of this, it can be almost impossible to keep track of a user's identity, geophysical location, or even what their specific activities are.
High levels of anonymity	Criminals and cyberattackers on the dark web, and even legitimate users, try to keep their identity a secret – thus making it difficult to keep track of them.

(Continued)

User identities keep changing	The criminals and the cyberattackers on the dark web are constantly changing their identities – thus, it is very difficult for law enforcement officials and digital forensics experts to build up reliable profiles on these individuals and/or groups.
The difficulties of jurisdiction	Traditionally, law enforcement is done in the jurisdiction in which it happens. But in the dark web, with everything being hidden, especially the geophysical location, it is nearly impossible to determine which law enforcement agency has control over what on the dark web. Thus, this could make the collect-ability and preservation of evidence even more questionable.
It takes highly skilled professionals	Trying to track criminals and cyberattackers on the dark web requires that the law enforcement officials get into their actual mindset. The only way to truly do this is to hire people who have turned from the "Bad Side" to the "Good Side" – but in the end, how trusting can they really be?
Evidence collected comes in different formats	Once a digital forensics team gets involved in collecting evidence on the dark web, one of the key challenges that arise is that there is no set of best standards or practices which allow for it to be admissible in a court of law without any question.
Tracebacking becomes more difficult	This is the process of where any type or kind of illicit activities or transactions can be traced back to its source. While this may be a relatively easier task to do on the public Internet because of the availability of resources, this is far more difficult to do on the dark web.

What Is Actually Down There

The Other Search Engines

Although the DuckDuckGo seems to be a rather popular search engine for the dark web, there are some others as well, which are as follows:

1. The Hidden Wiki: As its name implies, there is a version of Wikipedia that has been created solely for the dark web. With this portal, you can actually access different websites that are available on the dark web. Unlike the Wikipedia that is available on the public web, many of the search results that are returned back to you are actually garbled, and in a way, rather meaningless. For example, instead of giving you a valid domain, only alphanumeric text (which consists primarily of integers and letters all mixed up together), but the Hidden Wiki will take you to these sites. But be cautioned, be extremely careful of what you actually click on. For example, it does not simply search for those websites that are actually legal. It will also search and index those websites which are extremely nefarious in nature. And in fact, yes, there are even spoofed up versions of the Hidden Wiki on the dark web as well.

2. Searx: This is also deemed to be a rather "safe" search engine to use on the dark web. In fact, in some ways, it is even deemed to be more powerful than Google, as you can create search queries that are even much more granular. For example, you can build out these queries on the following permutations:
   - Various different files;
   - Certain images;
   - Maps;
   - All flavors of different music styles;

- News and science;
- Videos;
- Social media posts across **_all of the platforms_** that are currently available.

In fact, this search engine has been deemed to be more robust in returning results to you that are safe and legal to visit.

3. <u>Daniel</u>: This is also yet another search engine that you can use in the dark web that is closely related to the Searx. For example, there are well over 7,000 links that have already been indexed, which will help you get more refined searches as you enter your query keywords into this search engine. Another very unique functionality of the Daniel search engine is that it will actually notify you if a website that you want to visit on the dark web is actually online and available. The primary advantage of this is that you don't have to spend waste hours combing through each website to see if it is real or not. Another rule of thumb here: As it was mentioned, you don't want to stay of the dark web for a very long period of time – just for your own safety.

The Available Resources Worth Taking a Look at

In the public Internet, while the freedom of speech and expression for the most part is protected, there are certain geographic regions around the world where this is strictly forbidden. Therefore, there are many individuals, and even business entities, that create specialized forums and websites so that they can express their views freely, without the fear of censorship.

In a way, this can be considered a good aspect of the dark web. But even then, one still has to be careful, because even a website and/or forum that has been created with good intentions can still be spoofed into a malicious one. So in this regard, here are some other websites that are available for accessing and viewing on the dark web:

1. Facebook: Believe it or not, there is another version of this that lurks down there. One can create an anonymous account, in order to help protect their identity. But given how stealthy people are on the dark web, this probably will not last for too long. This "other version" of Facebook has been created for the sole purpose of avoiding censorship, as just discussed.

    a. The haven for Bitcoins: Many people very often have the notion that Bitcoin and other virtual currencies are relatively new. While this may be true on the public Internet, it is far from it on the dark web. They have been in existence for many years and are what used to conduct financial transactions. The reason for this is simple: You never want to pay with a credit card, check, or even cash on the dark web. Not only is this the prime way to steal your identity but law enforcement will have a much easier time tracking your movements. By paying with a virtual currency, your anonymity remains relatively intact.

    b. BBC News: This famous news outlet also has its own website on the dark web. The idea here is to also avoid censorship in those countries where it is banned. Here, people can freely access news stories and share thoughts, ideas, and comments. The news is not just restricted to that is happening in the United Kingdom, it covers events that happen on a global basis.

2. A place for investigative journalism: Probably one of the more famous portals for this is known as "ProPublica", as it maintains a rather strong presence on the public Internet as well. In this regard, investigative journalism can thrive as much as it can, because with being on the dark web, people and groups can pretty much post

anything they want to, or even provide evidence for an ongoing, investigative story that is going on. Another news portal that is similar in this regard is known as "SecureDrop". This includes specific place witnesses (aka "whistleblowers") that can meet with investigative journalists in order to share what they know while still remaining anonymous. In fact, some of the largest news entities have even formed their own SecureDrop websites on the dark web, and examples of this include the following:

■ Forbes;
■ Reuters;
■ The Financial Times.

The Communication Services

Yes, there are even various modes of communication on the dark web. Probably one of the most favored ones is that of posting on forums. But there is no guarantee of anonymity here. So, in an effort to do this, various email services have thus emerged. A sampling of these are as follows:

1. ProtonMail: This is an email software package that was actually developed in Switzerland. This has been deemed to be one of the most robust and secure email services that is available for use on the dark web. In fact, if you set up an account with them, you do not have to provide any sort of personal or confidential information about yourself. It has been designed to work in conjunction with the Tor Web Browser, thus making it more difficult for people to track your movements on the dark web – but keep in mind that there is no guarantee in this either.
2. SecMail: This is another email service that is just as almost as popular as ProtonMail. The only drawback

here is that you are allocated only 25 Mb of storage space.

3. <u>Zero Bin</u>: This email package has been designed specifically for the dark web, but it also contains a chatting mechanism. What is nice about this is that after you have copied and pasted any content, it gets automatically encrypted; and the content of your email/chat message can also be protected with any type of password that you choose to create (of course, if it is long with alphanumeric values, the better it will be).

The Difficulties That Law Enforcement Has on the Dark Web

We also examined some of the difficulties that law enforcement and digital forensics experts face when trying to collect evidence, especially those of a latent nature. But given just how things have been evolving from the standpoint of technology, especially driven by the COVID-19 pandemic, collecting this evidence has not only become even more difficult but also become even more time-consuming. The end result of all of this is that it now takes a much longer time to bring a perpetrator to justice.

This is further substantiated by a recent study that was conducted by the RAND Corporation and the Police Executive Research Forum. Their findings include the following:

■ The very small pieces of digital evidence such as Bitcoins are very difficult to track down. But they are needed, as they can be linked to other, much larger pieces of latent evidence.
■ Because the cyberattacker now uses a myriad of sophisticated tools when they are on the dark web, it is very difficult for experts to build a comprehensive profile on them.

- Trying to prove the authenticity of digital evidence that is "anonymized" can prove to be a very laborious process, with no guarantees that it would be admissible in a court of law, even if the most minute trace of legitimacy can be ascertained.
- As mentioned, just about everything on the dark web is encrypted to some degree or another. As a result, this makes that much more difficult to capture any digital evidence on a real-time basis. The only way this can be done is by actually "jailbreaking" into the physical RAM of the server that is hosting a targeted website in order to collect this kind of evidence, and yet maintaining its integrity at the same time.
- It is very difficult for digital forensics investigators and law enforcement officials to actually break into a particular device in order to collect evidence. This is best exemplified by Apple and the FBI. On a number of instances, the FBI could not break into the security features of the iPhone, and Apple refused to cooperate and help in this regard. Their claim was that it would invade not only the privacy rights of the individual in question but would also give their trade secrets when it came to their encryption algorithms.
- The various marketplaces on the dark web in which illicit transactions are very often hardened. Thus, it makes it even more difficult to collect any latent pieces of digital evidence.
- Once one piece of digital evidence has been found, it is often difficult to find other pieces that relate to it, thus making it even harder to build a case against an alleged perpetrator.
- The use of cryptocurrencies often hinders the process of tracking down the cyberattacker. For example, they could use Bitcoin in one marketplace, but yet use an entirely different one in another marketplace.

The Emergence of Supply Chain Attacks – SolarWinds

Every day there always seems to be a hacking story that takes place. Some make the news headlines, and some don't. Probably some of the biggest ones that took place pre-COVID-19 were the Sony, British Airways website, and the Marriott Group hacks. During the pandemic, of course, the threat vectors exploded like nothing ever seen before, but there is one hack that totally gripped the world – which is the SolarWinds security breach.

The reason why this hack gained so much attention was the magnitude of it, and especially the entities that were involved and those that were affected. For example, you have the Russians that were primarily blamed for it, and then on the other side of this, you have Microsoft and some of the largest federal government agencies, such as the Department of Defense (DoD) that were gravely impacted by it.

How IT Was All Triggered

First, SolarWinds is a rather large software company that creates and deploys network monitoring tools. These are primarily used by larger companies in Corporate America, especially by Managed Service Providers (MSPs) that keep an eye on the IT and network infrastructures for their clients.

Through this, any sort or type of anomalies can be detected in the network flow of traffic, and any corrective actions can be taken immediately, which is often done remotely. One of these tools that are manufactured by SolarWinds is known as "Orion".

It is important to note at this point that this kind of hack is different from the others that we are accustomed to hearing about. Specifically, this is known as a "Supply Chain Attack".

This simply means that rather than breaking into digital assets of SolarWinds, other third parties were targeted that made use of the Orion software package.

With this kind of approach, the cyberattacker was thus able to breach into the lines of defense of many other private and public entities.

For example, in this situation, over 30,000 entities were impacted on a global basis. Now the question is, what was the main point of entry by which all of this havoc was created? Well, back in December 2020, many of SolarWinds' customers that made use of Orion already had deployed two major software updates to it. But what were thought to be system patches were actually pieces of nefarious malware, disguised to look like legitimate and safe downloads.

Even more bewildering is the fact that the cyberattackers already had gained access to the software development platforms that created these updates going back as far as October 2019. They were able to access them through the gaps and vulnerabilities that were present in the many Microsoft Office 365 that the employees of SolarWinds made use of on a daily basis.

So, once the cyberattackers were in and were able to stay that way without going unnoticed, they then examined some of the best ways in which they could cause the maximum amount of damage that was possible. They determined that inserting Trojan Horses into these platforms would be the best way to accomplish this goal.

So, in March 2020, the insertion of these malicious payloads started to take place, which would become known as "SUNBURST". But apart from this, the cyberattackers also created various backdoors in these payloads that would communicate with third-party servers over which they had control over.

From here, any PII datasets of both employees and customers could be covertly hijacked, and either be sold on the dark web for a rather nice profit or be used to launch subsequent identity theft attacks.

But what was even worst is that these malicious payloads, backdoors, and Trojan Horses actually appeared to be legitimate modifications to the software patches and upgrades that were ultimately downloaded by the many business and government entities that made use of the Orion system. Now, the next question is how could this level of believability actually be established, and why did it take so long to discover?

Well, the various types of malicious payloads were inserted into the "SolarWinds.Orion.Core.BusinessLayer.dll". These are the dynamic-link libraries (DLLs) which were created for the software patches and upgrades exclusively for Orion. In order to get through, these DLLs were signed by digital certificates that verified their authenticity but were also covertly tampered with. To make matters even worse, these DLLs were designed to be dormant for a period of 14 days, so that any confidential information could be easily transmitted back to the third-party servers.

Even FireEye, one of the largest cybersecurity firms in the world, was also impacted by this. Other affected entities include the following:

■ Microsoft;
■ Intel;
■ Cisco;
■ Belkin;
■ The Department of Homeland Security;
■ The Department of the Treasury;
■ The Department of Commerce;
■ The Department of State;
■ The Department of Energy;
■ The US Nuclear Security Administration.

It is also quite possible that other businesses and government agencies could have also been impacted.

What Has Been Learned?

Given the large scope of this breach, there are many key takeaways an IT security can apply, but the following are some of the big ones:

1. <u>Always know where your source code is coming from</u>: The malicious payload was inserted into the various DDLs and then masqueraded as a legitimate software/ upgrade to the Orion platform. In this instance, it is unlikely that any kind of tests was conducted in the source code of the software to make sure that there was no malware in them before they were deployed onto the customer's IT/network infrastructure. Had this been done, it is quite probable that this kind of attack could have been stopped in its tracks, or at the very least, the damage that it created could have been contained. Therefore, it is crucial that CISOs take a proactive approach in testing all forms of source code (for example, whether it is used in creating a Web app or software patch) to remediate any gaps and vulnerabilities before they are released out to the production environment.

2. <u>Vetting out of third parties</u>: The SolarWinds security breach has been technically referred to as a "Supply Chain Attack". This simply means that the cyberattackers took advantage of the vulnerabilities of third parties that SolarWinds made use of in order to inflict the maximum damage possible. This underscores the importance of one of the most basic rules: Always vet your suppliers before you hire and onboard one. This means that as a CISO, you need to make sure that your IT security is carefully scrutinizing the security procedures and policies of that particular third party that you are thinking of outsourcing some of your business functions to. It must be on par with what you have in place in your organization, or even better than that. But simply making sure of

what your potential supplier has put into place in terms of controls is not a one-time deal. Even after you have hired and have a business relationship with them, you need to make sure that they are strictly enforcing these controls on a regular basis. This can take place by conducting a security audit. In the end, if your supplier becomes a victim of a cyberattack, and the PII datasets you have entrusted are breached, ***you will be held legally and financially responsible, not them***.

3. <u>Keep things simple and easy to track</u>: It is simply human nature to think that investing in a large amount of security tools and technologies means that you will be immune from a security breach. But in reality, this is far from the truth. In fact, taking this proverbial "Safety In Numbers" approach simply expands the attack surface for the hacker, which was experienced in the SolarWinds breach. Instead, it is far wiser to invest in perhaps five firewalls versus ten of them, but making sure that they are strategically deployed to where they are needed the most. By using this kind of methodology, not only will your IT security team be able to filter out those threats that are real, but you will also be able to pinpoint the entry point of the cyberattacker in a much quicker fashion, versus the time it took SolarWinds, simply due to the fact of the overload of tools and technologies they had in place. Because of this, it took literally months before anybody realized that something was wrong. In this regard, you may even want to make use of both AI and ML tools. With this kind of automation in place, false positives will be a thing of the past, and those alerts and warnings that are legitimate and for real will be triaged and escalated in a much quicker time frame.

4. <u>Make use of segmentation</u>: In today's environment, many businesses are now seriously considering of adopting what is known as the Zero Trust Framework. This is the

kind of methodology where absolutely nobody is trusted in both the internal and external environments. Further, any individual wishing to gain access to a particular shared resource must be authenticated through at least three or more layers of authentication. But apart from this, another critical component of this is the creation of what are known as "Subnets". With this, you are breaking up your entire network infrastructure into smaller ones. But what is key here is that each of these subnets has its own layer of defense, so it becomes almost statistically impossible for a cyberattacker to break through each and every layer. SolarWinds did not take this approach with their network infrastructure, so as a result, the cyberattackers were able to get in through the first time around.

5. Update your security technologies: With the advent of the remote workforce, the traditional security tools such as the VPN have started to reach their breaking points, and thus their defensive capabilities. Because of this, it is important that you consider upgrading these systems to what is known as the NGFW. These kinds of technologies are now becoming much more robust in ascertaining malicious data packets that are both entering and leaving your network infrastructure. SolarWinds did not invest properly in these kinds of upgrades, so therefore, the cyberattackers were able to penetrate through the weaknesses of the VPNs that they were making use of.

References

1. https://www.thecut.com/2020/04/what-is-zoombombing.html
2. https://www.itproportal.com/news/thousands-of-malicious-covid-19-domains-hosted-on-public-clouds/
3. https://www.pcmag.com/news/a-third-of-remote-workers-say-weak-internet-has-hurt-their-productivity
4. https://www.upguard.com/blog/cybersecurity-risk

5. https://www.itgovernance.co.uk/cyber-resilience
6. https://xgrcsoftware.com/what-is-vendor-compliance-management/
7. https://blogs.gartner.com/smarterwithgartner/a-better-way-to-manage-third-party-risk/
8. https://www.emotiv.com/glossary/data-privacy/
9. https://www.forcepoint.com/cyber-edu/data-security
10. https://www.paloaltonetworks.com/cyberpedia/what-is-sase#:~:text=SASE%20is%20the%20convergence%20of,%2C%20cloud%2Ddelivered%20service%20model.&text=This%20approach%20allows%20organizations%20to,applications%20or%20devices%20are%20located.

Chapter 3

How to Prepare for the Next Pandemic

Introduction

So far, we have covered topics from the molecular constructs of the novel COVID-19 virus to the cybersecurity lessons that have been garnered from this pandemic. This is no doubt a once-in-a-lifetime event, and this is something that nobody ever wants to be repeated, for obvious reasons.

But if something like this were to happen again, whether it is a pandemic, a large-scale cyberattack on critical infrastructure, or even a natural disaster, what can be done by the CISO and his or her IT security team to better prepare for this?

This is the focal point of this chapter of this book. While a business must work together as one harmonic unit in order to move forward after they have been hit, this chapter specifically addresses what needs to be done from the standpoint of cybersecurity. Thus, the following topics will be covered:

- The need for incident response, disaster recovery, and business continuity plans;
- The need for effective penetration testing;
- The importance of threat hunting;
- The need for endpoint security;
- The need to use the SOAR model;
- The need for security information and event management (SIEM) usage;
- The importance of the Zero Trust Framework.

In other words, this chapter of the book reviews the tools and the methodologies that the CISO and his or her IT security team need to have in place if or when the next massive wave of novel COVID-19 infections hit.

The Need for an Incident Response Plan

Very oftern, there is confusion as to what incident response/ disaster recovery (DR)/business is really about. Frequently, these three are all used together interchangeably, but in reality, they are quite different. In this first section of this book, we cover what incident response is. It can be technically defined as follows:

> An incident response plan ensures that in the event of a security breach, the right personnel and procedures are in place to effectively deal with a threat. Having an incident response plan in place ensures that a structured investigation can take place to provide a targeted response to contain and remediate the threat

(Source: 4.)

The rest of this section details what should go into the incident response plan.

The Incident Response Plan

In today's world, cyber threats and attacks are becoming the norm. There is not one single business or corporation that is immune from these threats. It seems like that no matter how much an entity does to fortify its defense perimeters, the cyberattacker will find a way to circumvent it and inflict whatever possible damage that he or she can do.

Such kinds of attacks can range from the theft of confidential information and data about your customers to launching extremely sophisticated ransomware attacks, in which Bitcoin is the only acceptable form of "ransom payment". Consider some of these statistics:

■ Over 70% of business entities have reported that they have been a victim of a major cyberattack in just the past 12 months;
■ The automotive industry reported a 32% increase in detected incidents;
■ There was a 60% increase in security breaches in the healthcare sector alone;
■ There was also an astounding 527% increase in cyber-related incidents in the power and utility industry.

These statistics further substantiate the fact cyberattacks can occur in any industry. Now, consider some of the financial losses that are associated with this:

■ The average cost of a single corporate data breach reached $3.5 million, an increase of 15%;
■ Each record that is hijacked or stolen from a database costs a business on average $145.10.

The unfortunate truth is that many cyberattacks are so covert and stealthy that they can often go unnoticed for a long period of time.

However, it is important to note that responding to an incident as soon as it has been discovered becomes absolutely crucial. The above definition states that a process must be used, but it must be a defined and orderly one.

For example, there must be a clear line of communication, specific roles and duties must be assigned to each team member of the Incident Response (IR) team, but most importantly, there must be a mechanism put into place which allows the IR team members to report back as to what they have discovered. From here, then the next action items can be quickly determined and enacted upon.

In other words, the IR process must detail how to handle just about any type or kind of cyberattack. This process must be viewed as literally an emergency plan (such as a step by step policy) in order to increase the chances that a business entity will be able to resume back to normal operations in a quick and efficient manner. This process can be diagrammed as follows:

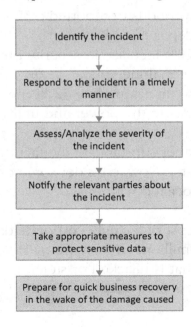

The Risks and the Needs Associated Going Offline

When a business or a corporation is hit by a cyberattack, one of the first questions that often gets asked is just how much the IT infrastructure has been damaged, or even if the cyber-attacker is still lurking around trying to infect other systems in the process of confusion and mayhem. It is in these instances that the thought of shutting down the entire IT infrastructure or just parts of it in order to prevent further damage comes to mind.

While this might be a tempting option to utilize, there are certain risks that are inherent with doing this, as this is often considered one of the most drastic scenarios to take. For example, in a complete shutdown, information and data might be lost that may never be recovered.

Or, if the software development team is working on a mission-critical application for a customer, this could mean that the source code could be lost, thus resulting in a much-delayed delivery once the operations have been restored back to normal. A complete shutdown would greatly impact not only the entire organization, but also its customers, especially if they are depending upon mobile apps in order to conduct their daily activities.

A direct shutdown can also mean that any forensics evidence could also be lost, thus greatly impeding any subsequent investigations.

Shutting down any systems, or going offline, is greatly dependent upon the magnitude of the cyberattack which has just occurred, and the systems and processes that are being directly impacted. This is not a decision to be taken lightly, as sometimes it may have to be made in just a matter of minutes.

For instance, if the IT staff could quickly calculate the risk of any downtime incurred versus the time it would take to just remedy an infected system. If it is discovered that the situation can be quickly patched and there is no sensitive data that has been impacted, then there is no need to go offline.

But this is not the only permutation to take into consideration. There are others that can be taken into account by mere observation of the server logs. For example, if it was discovered that a cyberattacker is trying to gain access to just a certain network component of the IT infrastructure, then a partial shutdown is warranted in order to prevent this unauthorized access from occurring. In this regard, a partial shutdown is a much more preferable and less drastic approach to take than a complete shutdown.

But there are those instances where a complete shutdown might be needed. For instance, if the cyber-attack involved the use of malware or worms, these can be spread very quickly to other systems and can literally bring an organization to its knees. In order to prevent this from happening, it may be decided quickly to go completely offline in order to prevent the malware or the worms from causing further damage by spreading itself.

Thus, determining which systems and processes need to be shut down or brought offline is also a direct function of their level of importance to a business or corporation. This is best ascertained by conducting a business impact analysis, also known as a "BIA".

This document will help to quantify the exact level of the importance of these assets, what they are used for, and the impact they will have on to have an organization if they are indeed brought offline. The BIA can thus be used to determine if an impacted area of the IT infrastructure can just be protected while a patch is being quickly developed, or if it is better to take that particular area either partially or completely offline.

It is important to note that this decision is a combination of considering both quantitative and qualitative variables; there is no hard and fast rule for making it, and it will be unique to each and every business and corporation.

The Benefits and the Needs for Fast Time to Detect and Time to Respond Periods

When an organization is hit by a cyberattack, the IT staff obviously needs to respond as quickly as possible to the incident. Any wasted time will simply translate more down-time in the end, which will mean lost revenue, brand recognition damage, and worst of all lost customers. Thus, the need for an orderly and precise incident response plan is a must, and this will be discussed in more detail later in this chapter.

But, responding as quickly as possible to a cyberattack also brings about some benefits to it. Some of these are as follows:

1. The downtime, if any, will be minimized. Therefore, the business or the corporation will be able to come back to full operations quickly, assuming that there is a proper incident response plan put into place and that all sensitive data has been backed up properly and can be accessed efficiently and quickly. The end result is that, depending upon the severity of the cyberattack, the financial bottom line of the company should not be too greatly impacted. Also, responding quickly to an incident will mean that any vulnerabilities that have exploited by the cyberattacker will be minimized and also reduce the risk of the same incident happening to a different part of the organization.

2. Quickly responding to a cyber threat and immediately notifying your customers as to what happened could in the long run, actually win new business. For example, when you communicate to your customer in a timely manner, it shows to them that not only do you take your due diligence seriously, but that you also care about them on a much more personal level. In fact, this is where many organizations fail, because many customers do not know they too have become a victim until a

much later in point in time. In these instances, very often a letter is mailed out, thus leaving an "impersonal effect". So, the manner and the timeframe in which a customer is contacted can also make a huge difference. A phone call to the customer from a member of the management team shortly after an incident has taken place would leave a much more "personalized effect"; it will prove to them that by taking the time and effort to use this mode of communication, you take their security very seriously as well. Thus, in the end, this personal touch will create a much more favorable and long-lasting impression to the customer, which could bring in more repeat as well as a referable business later on.

3. After an organization has been hit by a cyberattack, one of the key areas that will be looked into by management is filing a claim with the respective insurance company in order to be compensated for the associated costs incurred with restoring business operations. Showing your agent that you responded quickly to the incident by having a well-crafted incident response plan will not only mean that you will receive your claim money quickly, but you could also receive policy discounts in the future.

4. By responding in a timely manner to any kind of security breach, this will allow for a thorough investigation to follow in an expedient fashion as well. This will mean that evidence will still be fresh and intact, thus allowing for any forensics information and data to be collected quickly as well. This of course translates into evidence that will be admissible in a court of law, and which can also be used to bring the cyberattacker to justice.

5. Typically, after a cyberattack, the larger corporations and businesses (such as those in the Fortune 500) might be required to release what is known as "Electronically Stored Information" or "ESI" in short, to the Federal Regulatory Authorities and Law Enforcement Agencies. The quicker that an organization can respond to a

security-related incident, the greater the chances that the ESI will remain intact and can be produced quickly when questioned. Any delays in this regard by the entity could result in very stiff fines and penalties by the authorities.

6. Responding quickly to a cyberattack will create a subsequent, proactive security mindset among the IT staff of any kind of organization, large or small. This in turn will lead to what is known as a "Targeted Security Monitoring" environment. This occurs when the IT staff can identify many types of cyber threat vectors before they increase in their degree of severity, thus giving you a greater chance of mitigating them in the future. With a reactive security mindset, not only will incident response time be much slower, but you will be forced to devote all of your resources in figuring out what exactly is transpiring to just one incident, thus leaving the organization much more vulnerable to being exposed to other cyberattacks at the same time.

Responding quickly to security incident means also that the right team needs to be put into place as well at the business or corporation. The following matrix illustrates who should be involved in responding to an incident:

Title	Role
Team Leader	Responsible for the overall incident response; will coordinate the necessary actions that need to take place.
Incident Lead	Responsible for coordinating the actual response.
IT Contact	Responsible for communications between the Incident lead and other members of the IT staff.

(Continued)

Title	Role
Legal Representative	Responsible for leading the legal aspects of the incident response.
Public Relations Officer	Responsible for protecting and promoting the image of the business entity during an incident response.
Management Team	Responsible for approving and directing security policy during an incident response.

The Importance of Communications in Incident Response

Just as much as it is important to have a clearly defined incident response plan and having the incident response team in place, the lines of communication are also equally important. Responding to a cyberattack can be chaotic enough, and this does not need to be made worse by not communicating with the members of the incident response in a clear and succinct fashion. After all, reducing the downtime as much as possible is one of the key goals of incident response, and any improper communications can only further exacerbate a tense situation even more. The importance of effective incidence response communications (also known as the "Crisis Communications Plan") encompasses three key areas:

1. Communications Internal to the business or corporation: By maintaining open lines of communication, this will help to minimize the risk of any sensitive information from being inadvertently released to third parties. Any unauthorized release of information could impede any subsequent investigation. It will also serve as a vehicle to minimize any rumors or speculation.

One of the best methods to have good communications is to ensure that each part of the incident response plan covers how information and data will be relayed among the team members that are responsible for that specific component of the plan. For example, the mechanisms that will be used to communicate with each other need to be clearly defined. For example:

- Will there be a central hotline for the team members to call into?
- Will there be a main command center from which all communications will be centralized and then dispersed among the incident response team members?
- What will be the main vehicle(s) of communications – wireless devices, Smartphones, etc.? Will each member of the incident response team have a dedicated device for IR communications, or will their current work-issued device(s) be sufficed enough?
- What will be the form of communications? For instance, will it be Email, actual phone conversations, text messages, instant messages, etc.?
- How often will these lines of communications be tested in order to ensure that they will work quickly and efficiently when they are needed?

2. Communications for Compliance-Related Issues: After a cyberattack has occurred, a business or corporation now has to formally report to the federal authorities what exactly has happened, the extent of the damage that was caused, and which parties were impacted (for instance, customers, suppliers, other third-party vendors, etc.). If there is a time delay or failure to report this, it is quite possible that the organization could face severe financial penalties. In other words, this aspect of the IR communications process should be a part of the planning process, instead of making it a reactionary one.

In this aspect, the legal department from the organization must also be included. For example, they can assist in determining how the affected parties should be notified, and how exactly the security breach should be communicated. This aspect is very important, so that a violation of any regulatory or privacy requirements does not actually occur.

3. <u>Communications with the Media</u>: In this aspect, the public relations department needs to be involved in any incident response communications. They can act as a conduit for building up a good rapport with the local and state law enforcement agencies when reporting the occurrence of a cyberattack. They can also help prepare the proper documents that are needed to relay information to the public such as press releases, announcements, and other forms of disclosure statements. It is also important to have a member of the IT staff be involved in this part of the IR communications process, so that they help break down all of the so called "techno-jargon" into a language that will be easily and clearly understood by the public. It is important to note that the documents here will not contain each and every aspect of what exactly has transpired; therefore, it is crucial that the two sides (the designated PR and IT staff members) from the organization work together in a harmonious fashion to help ensure that the information which is communicated to the public is not taken out of context.

The bottom line is that by having effective incident response communications, an organization could actually win praise among customers, investors, regulatory agencies, and even the public by being open, honest, and forthright in a timely manner after it has been impacted by a cyberattack.

In summary, the key benefits of effective incident response communications are as follows:

- It will help to increase an overall sense of heighted security awareness among the employees of the organization;
- It can help to mitigate the degree of severity of a cyberattack;
- It can help reduce the time it takes to respond to a cyberattack;
- It can help the business entity identify a threat before it actually happens;
- It will help to remind employees of the organization as to what matters most in a crisis situation. For example:
  - We care about our investors and customers;
  - We are responding to the cyberattack in a quick and timely fashion;
  - We will cooperate with investigative authorities to determine what happened and who did it.

The Incident Response Communications (Crisis Communications) Plan

As we have discussed that the three key areas in quick incident response are critical, it is at this point that crafting the actual incident communications plan becomes crucial. It is important to note that each plan will be very unique to a business or a corporation; therefore, the exact requirements that need to go into such a plan will vary.

In these instances, it could prove to be very beneficial for an organization to actually hire an outside company that specializes in creating such plans. The biggest advantage of this is that the incident response communications plan will be created from an unbiased and neutral perspective.

But, the general components that should be included in this plan should include the following:

- Identify who will be specifically involved on the incidence response communications team: In this component of the plan, it is very crucial that the right people from all of the departments of the business or corporation are selected. Once selected, all of these individuals must then understand the gravity of their responsibilities, as they must be able to respond quickly at a moment without hesitation. The key individuals that need to be included in this team are the following:

■ The CEO, CFO, and the CIO or CISO;
■ A representative from the Public Relations department;
■ A representative from the Investor Relations department;
■ A representative from the Human Resources department;
■ A representative from the Sales and Marketing department.

It is also important that at least two individuals from these respective departments should be trained in how to handle any communications or queries from the media. Also, an alternate to each representative should be picked in case the primary representative cannot be reached during the time of a crisis.

■ Have mechanisms in place where employees can help communicate any unforeseen threats: In this regard, there should be an open line of communications where feedback from employees is solicited across all departments of the organization and at all levels. The goal here is to have the ability to report any new threats and even new ideas for the continuous refinement of the incident response communications process to the appropriate representative of the IR communications team (as described). By having this particular line of communications in place, a proactive security mindset will thus be instilled among all employees of the business or corporation.

■ <u>Create and develop the messaging around the risks that</u> <u>have been identified</u>: After the representatives have been selected and the open lines of communications set forth, the next step is to create the messaging for each kind of cyber risk that the organization is prone to. Obviously, the details of what will be communicated to the public and other key stakeholders will vary if an organization is actually hit by a cyberattack. But at this point in the incident response communications plan, it is important to have at least the messaging template prepared so that the designated representatives of the various departments will be able to communicate with confidence and effectiveness.

■ <u>Create the internal contact roster</u>: This component of the incident response communications plan is deemed to be one of the most important. After all, once a business or corporation is hit by a cyberattack, the first thing that will come to mind is contacting the department representatives to determine exactly what is happening and to what degree the damage is. In this regard, it becomes critical to have all of the contact information (which includes work Email, personal Email, work cell number, personal cell number, and even home telephone number) for each of the department representatives. All of this contact information should be documented in an easy and quick-to-read format, such as that of a call tree. Also, it is important to include all of this contact information for the alternate department representative. The bottom line here is that all of the contact information must be up to date and confirmed at least once a month for any changes.

■ <u>Identify and establish relationships with the key stake-</u> <u>holders of the organization</u>: Apart from communicating with employees and the department representatives, it is also equally important to reach out to the stakeholders that have a vested interest in the well-being of the organization in the time of a crisis. Such individuals include the following:

■ Investors and shareholders;
■ Customers and business partners;
■ Suppliers and distributors;
■ Any relevant government official at the local level.

This particular component of the incident response communications plan is an often overlooked one; therefore, it is important to include all of their contact information in the call tree as well. The call tree should be made available to all department representatives (including their alternates) and key stakeholders in printed, electronic, and online formats.

Finally, it is important for a business or a corporation to not focus on just preparing for just one type or kind of cyberattack. Rather, a holistic view should be taken, which will thus allow you to prepare for ***any*** cyberattack.

These components of the incident response communications plan can be diagrammed as follows:

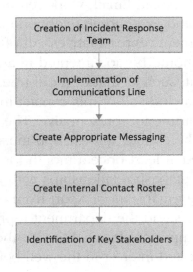

How to Report a Security Incident to Internal Stakeholders

As discussed throughout this chapter, the need to respond quickly and to communicate on a real-time basis after an organization has been hit by a cyberattack is very critical. Also, the need to communicate after the cyberattack has been specifically identified and its effects have been resolved.

After this, people will want to know what exactly has happened, the damages and/or losses it has created, and what can and will be done in the future to prevent this attack and similar attacks.

In these instances, it is imperative to communicate all of this to parties that are both internal to the business or corporation (such as the employees, executives, board of directors, investors – these are considered to the "internal stakeholders") and external (such as the partners, clients, suppliers, distributors, etc. – these are considered to the "external stakeholders").

Thus, withholding any kind of information about the cyberattack could lead to a serious level of mistrust and misunderstandings. Therefore, the representatives of the incident response team have to open and investigate as to what exactly transpired.

How this information will be ultimately disseminated to the internal stakeholders is entirely up to the organization – there is no hard-and-fast rule for this. For instance, it could take place as a memo, an Email, or even be posted on the company intranet.

But in the end, perhaps having an open forum where the internal stakeholders are physically present could be the best venue to take. Following this approach will allow providing real-time questions/answers and also the internal stakeholders will feel that their input and suggestions will be valued and taken seriously.

But, in order to decide what will be formally communicated to the internal stakeholders, the following process is defined:

1. Triage the situation: The three fundamental questions about the cyberattack must be first answered. These are also known as the four "W's":
   - Who specifically launched the cyberattack?
   - Why did the cyberattack happen (in other words, what was the underlying motive)?
   - What parts of the organization did the cyberattack effect?
   - Where was the cyberattack launched from?
2. Decide the specific medium in which the internal stakeholders will be notified: As mentioned, this could take place either in a print, electronic, or direct person approach. But whatever the decided medium is, it is important that all messages (such as Emails and texts) be kept within the incident response team until the above questions have been fully answered.
3. Manage the timing of the communication: In this step, the internal stakeholders need to be told the venue of how they will be informed of the cyberattack and when such communications will actually occur.
4. Rehearse the message: At this stage, it will be important to conduct a dress rehearsal of the actual message that will be communicated among the internal stakeholders. For example, if it is in a print or electronic form, it will be important that all members of the incident response team review it carefully before it is distributed. Or, if it will be open forum based, then the presentation that will be given needs to be practiced, as well as the question/answer session, where it will be important to brainstorm any potential items that could be questioned by the internal stakeholders.

How to Report a Security Incident to External Stakeholders

The external stakeholders of the business or corporation are primarily your customers and also the suppliers and distributors who currently work with. It is the customer that drives revenue into your business, and if their confidential information or data (these include mostly credit card numbers, social security numbers, passwords, PIN numbers, etc.) has been compromised by a cyberattack, not only do you have a moral obligation to notify them as to what happened, but you also have a legal one.

This has been brought under the legislation known as the Data Security Breach Notification Act of 2015. This clearly states that an organization must take all precautions to protect customer data and inform them in a timely manner after a security breach has actually taken place.

It also requires entities to provide such notifications to all law enforcement and investigative branches at the federal, state, and local levels. If this is not done, a business or a corporation could face very harsh financial penalties and fines, and even criminal ones as well.

However, reporting a security breach to external stakeholders requires a different approach than reporting to internal stakeholders. This is primarily driven by the fact that the latter will be a much smaller group of people, versus the former, which will obviously be much larger.

As discussed earlier in this chapter, calling customers individually and notifying them as to what happened adds a "personal touch" in the communications process. Of course, this option is only feasible if you are a smaller business entity with a smaller customer base.

What protocols should be followed in notifying customers if you are a much larger business with thousands of customers? In these instances, sending out a letter to them in an expedient fashion would be the most prudent venue to take. But before the letters are drafted and sent off, very careful thought needs to be given as to how they will convey the message, that basically, their confidential information and data are at risk.

Here are the key areas that are to be considered:

1. Give very careful consideration to the tone and the voice of the letter: In these instances, it is important to keep the language of the letter as soft as possible. In other words, it should be kept to the point, no-nonsense, and easy to read and understand. This will help to reassure your customer base that you are looking after their best interests and that you will take care of them no matter how much effort is needed on your part.

2. Tell your customers exactly what happened: There is no need to reveal each and every bit of information, but your customers have a right to know as to what exactly transpired. This includes how the cyberattack occurred, what was impacted, and the severity of it, and what are the plans to prevent this from happening again. Most importantly, you need to tell your customers that you are working closely with investigators and law enforcement in order to track down your hijacked information/data before even further damage occurs (such as subsequent identity theft attacks). Also offer them free credit monitoring and identity theft protection. You are even important to include the relevant contact information so that they reach out to you with any concerns or questions.

3. Consider the audience of your customer base: If your business is large enough or virtual in nature, the chances are that you will probably have international customers. You may be thinking at this point, if they are in a different country, why should they be notified? The bottom line is that they are still your customer, and the fact still remains that their information and data resided on your servers; so

therefore, you still have a legal obligation to inform them that their information and data are at risk. Therefore, it will be important to draft a letter in their respective language. In this regard, hiring a translator in the respective a language is therefore a must. This will ensure that any nuances in the language translation will not cause any further misunderstandings.

4. <u>It must be understandable</u>: Just as it is important to communicate what exactly happened and what has been impacted by the cyberattack, it is also equally important that the letter be understandable to read. In other words, there is no need for the techno-jargon, keep the substantial portion (which is about the cyberattack) to use bold headings and bullet points. Try to keep this part down to just a couple of paragraphs. Remember, when a customer reads this kind of letter, they normally just skim it at first. Therefore, the importance of the letter and the gravity of the situation must be conveyed the first time your customers read the letter.

Finally, after the letter has been drafted into its final form, an attorney should also review it to make sure that it complies with the federal laws, as described previously in this subsection.

The Need for a Disaster Recovery Plan

This is a business owner's worst nightmare: Everything seems to be going well for a long period of time, and then all of a sudden, a disaster strikes, impacting your operations, your employees, and your customers. But given just how interconnected everything is today, there are also indirect parties that are all impacted, which include your suppliers and distributors, shareholders, families, contractors, any external third parties that you may outsource work to, your advisory board, and even the board of directors.

Depending upon the magnitude of the disaster, it could take a very long time to recover, and the need to come back to life as quickly as possible is of course of the utmost importance. But how does one go about this? This is of course no easy task to accomplish, but the process all begins with a very carefully crafted plan that can be launched and executed in just a matter of minutes.

This is where the role of a disaster recovery plan (DRP) comes into place, as it spells out the exact process of what needs to be done in order to bring up at least the mission-critical operations, then from there, the other processes that need to be redeployed.

Given the cyber threat landscape of today, this plan is becoming even more vital by the day. For instance, one just never knows when they will become the victim of the next cyberattacker, no matter how large or small it is. But given the sheer importance of disaster recovery planning, many businesses and corporations simply do not understand the magnitude of the potential dangers that they face.

Consider some of these statistics:

■ 58% of businesses are not prepared to handle data loss when disaster strikes;
■ 60% of the smaller- to medium-sized businesses (SMBs) that actually lose information and data will be forced to shut within a six-month time span;
■ There are over 140,000 hard drive failures in SMBs on a weekly basis without any plan in place in recovering the lost information and data;
■ Almost 30% of hard drive failures are caused by some sort of disaster, whether it is natural or cyber-related.

(Source: 2.)

It is important to keep in mind that creating a DRP can be a complex process as well as a huge undertaking. There is no cookie-cutter approach in doing this, and a lot depends upon the requirements of your own business. The goal of this chapter is to introduce you to the overall concept of a DRP. A subsequent chapter will provide further detail as to how you should go about creating and executing such a plan.

The Definition of a Disaster Recovery Plan

When one thinks of a disaster, the first thought that comes to mind is a cyberattack, ranging anywhere from ransomware to phishing, to Trojan Horses/malware/spyware to even social engineering. While this is the trend these days, a disaster can also include anything natural, such as a tornado, hurricane, or even a massive thunderstorm. The bottom line is that if your business is impacted in such a way that it needs to shut down in order to recover and bring up the mission-critical operations, you have been hit by a disaster. The question that is often thought of first is, "What exactly is a Disaster Recovery Plan?" It can be defined specifically as follows:

> A DRP is a business plan that describes how work can be resumed quickly and effectively after a disaster. Disaster recovery planning is just part of business continuity planning and applied to aspects of an organization that rely on an IT infrastructure to function.
>
> The overall idea is to develop a plan that will allow the IT department to recover enough data and system functionality to allow a business or organization to operate – even possibly at a minimal level.
>
> *(Source: 2.)*

Based on the definition above, a DRP is just that it is a comprehensive document or even a set of documents that lay out the needed steps in order to bring your business back up to the base level that is needed in order to conduct transactions and meet the immediate needs of customers. In fact, disaster recovery planning is just one part of a triad that needs to be taken into consideration when impacted.

The other two areas are:

- The Incident Response Plan: This plan provides details on how your business or corporation will respond to a disaster and mitigate any damage that is caused from it.
- The Business Continuity Plan: This also provides further details on how you will restore business operations for the longer term, after you have restored mission-critical operations (which is the goal of the DRP). In other words, this plan will bring your organization back up to speed to the point where it operated normally just before the disaster hit.

The Categories of Disaster

In creating your DRP, the following are three levels of disaster that you need to be aware of:

1. Minor disasters: These are the kinds of disasters which inflict just a minor financial damage to the business or corporation. For instance, it could be just a worm that has penetrated your IT infrastructure and has not really caused much of an impact other than just being a sheer nuisance or annoyance.
2. Major disasters: This is the type of disaster where a major portion of your IT infrastructure has been hit, impacting everything from the servers to the workstations and all types of wireless devices. Also, a huge amount of sensitive and proprietary customer information/data have been stolen or covertly hijacked. Your IT department and parts of your business simply cannot function in a normal fashion, and for all intents and purposes, they

will have to be shut down. This is the kind of cyberattack that most organizations are experiencing today.

3. <u>Catastrophic disasters</u>: This is the worst kind of disaster. In this kind of situation, the costs of restoring business operations far outweigh the benefits, and as a result, the organization will just have to simply shut down permanently. So far, this magnitude of cyberattack has not happened on a large scale yet but given the sophistication level of the cyberattacker these days, it is bound to happen sooner or later.

The Benefits of a Disaster Recovery Plan

Apart from restoring your mission-critical processes up in a short of period of time, a well-documented DRP has other numerous benefits, which include the following:

1. <u>Your organization will achieve greater cost efficiencies</u>: For example, before you can even engage in creating a DRP, you must first complete what is known as a "Business Impact Analysis" or a "BIA" in short. It is defined as follows:

   A business impact analysis (BIA) is the process of determining the criticality of business activities and associated resource requirements to ensure operational resilience and continuity of operations during and after a business disruption. The BIA quantifies the impacts of disruptions on service delivery, risks to service delivery, and recovery time objectives (RTOs) and recovery point objectives (RPOs). These recovery requirements are then used to develop strategies, solutions, and plans.

   (Source: 3.)

In other words, you are mapping out those IT assets that are at risk if and when a cyberattack actually occurs and quantifying that level of risk. From there, they will be categorized as:

■ High risk;
■ Medium risk;
■ Low risk.

By ascertaining this, you and your IT security team will know which and how many resources need to be dedicated to protecting those IT assets that are at most risk, thus resulting in an efficient spend of a tight IT budget.

2. <u>An increased level in worker productivity</u>: Believe it or not, a good DRP can actually improve the morale of your workforce, which will in turn increase their productivity levels. For example, when creating it, you will be assigning your employees various tasks that they must do in the face of a cyberattack. Knowing that they are making a positive impact in this fashion will only strengthen their belief that they are actually contributing to a greater good of the company, other than simply doing their daily job tasks.

3. <u>A happier customer base</u>: Because of all of the new cyberthreats that are coming out, as well as their variants, customers are becoming much more cautious in regard to opening any Emails that they receive, the links they click on, and even the websites that they visit. For example, although phishing remains one of the oldest attack vectors that is in existence, many cyberattackers are still using it in order to covertly hijack the personal identifiable information (PII) of unsuspecting victims. In other words, your customers want to know that they as a business owner, you are taking every precaution possible to protect their respective PIIs. By demonstrating that you have a solidified DRP in place, this will

only bolster their confidence to stay with you as customers and bring in repeat business. This means that
they feel safe and comforted knowing that in the unfortunate chance you are impacted by a cybersecurity
attack, and there are plans in place so that their PII will
not, as far as possible, fall into the hands of a cyberattacker.

4. <u>You will have a better sense of scalability</u>: After com-
pleting your business impact analysis (BIA) as previously described, you and your IT security team will
have a much greater understanding of the types of
resources that will be needed to protect them. Some of
these resources will be either based on premises, or in
the cloud, or perhaps even a combination of both.
Having such resources with the latter will offer your
organization a much greater realization of scalability.
For example, you can ramp up or ramp down very
quickly those resources, when an IT asset changes a
risk category. For example, if a "High Risk" asset
becomes downgraded to a "Medium Risk" categorization, those resources that were dedicated before can be
scaled down to meet the new requirements very
quickly. This will also help your organization in realiz-
ing greater cost efficiencies.

The Types of Disaster Recovery Plans

As mentioned before in this chapter, there is no "one size fits
all" DRP. Providing more details will depend upon your own
security requirements and needs. With that in mind, there is
yet another very important consideration that you need to
factor in creating your DR; and that is the kind of facility you
want to use to restore your mission-critical operations, and
eventually, your entire business.

The following are the types:

1. A cold site facility: This is where you rent out a secondary physical office location in which you can start to
   reestablish your business after you have been impacted
   by a cyberattack. These kinds of providers offer the tools
   that you need to get your servers up and running, which
   includes the proper levels of electrical power, cooling,
   and network connectivity. But, keep in mind that this
   kind of facility is bare-bones in nature in that you will
   have to install the new hardware, reinstall any existing
   software applications as well as your databases, and even
   upload your information and data once again from the
   backup tapes that you have used. As a result, this kind of
   approach can take a much longer time to restore critical
   business operations. Therefore, this option, while it is
   inexpensive from the outset, the costs can add up very
   quickly in just a short period of time.

2. A hot site facility: This is actually the opposite of the cold
   site facility, as just previously described. In this kind of
   scenario, the secondary office location is an exact replica
   of your existing IT infrastructure that you already have in
   place in your current business facility. This means that
   this facility is completely set up for you with regards to
   all of the software, hardware, and network connectivity
   that you will need to be up and running with crucial
   operations in just a matter of a couple of hours. This
   kind of set up even comes with all of the communications you will need in order to reach out to your teams
   between the hot site facility and your existing place of
   business, including all of the wireless devices you will
   need, and even full time technical support. In fact, all of
   your databases are also replicated at this facility, so
   reloading information and data is not even an issue. With
   a hot site facility, it is just like you walked into a new
   office setting as if nothing ever happened. While the

primary advantage of this is that there is virtually no downtime experienced in restoring operations, the main disadvantage is that this kind of set up can be extremely costly to a business.

3. <u>The cloud infrastructure</u>: In this kind of DR setup, you have your entire IT infrastructure outsourced to a cloud provider. In fact, this can be considered just like a hot site facility but rather than having a physical facility, it is all virtual, literally in the cloud. One of the key advantages of this is that you do not have to bear responsibility for any kind of hardware or software upgrades or licensing issues, it is all up to the cloud provider to do this for you. Also, they are responsible for keeping backups of all of the information and data that you have stored with them, as well as ensuring the latest security protocols have been implemented onto your virtual servers (also known as "Virtual Machines"). This kind of setup makes it that much easier to actually conduct a DR drill. These virtual machines can be replicated anywhere in just a matter of few seconds, so even creating backups of these should not be a problem. But best of all, the price is extremely affordable for any business: It is fixed and can be paid on a monthly basis. When in comparison to a cold site or a hot site facility, the costs of a cloud infrastructure are very nominal.

The Components of a Disaster Recovery Plan

There are many important items to a DRP, and each will have to be tailored to meet the needs of your business and requirements. In this section, we outline some of the key aspects that you should include in it:

1. <u>Create the disaster recovery team</u>: This is probably deemed to be one of the most crucial aspects of the DRP.

This will be the team of your employees that will be responsible for acting on their own areas in order to bring the business back up and running as quickly as possible after you have been hit by a cyberattack. This area should clearly detail the following:

- The team members who will be part of the actual DR team;
- Their specific responsibilities;
- Most importantly, their contact information. This should include work phone number, work Email address, home phone number, and even personal Email address as well. Also, make sure to include all cell phone numbers, both work and personal.

It is important to note the team members should include representatives from all of the departments that you may have. Depending upon how large the business is, upper management and even the C-Suite should also be included. Remember, clear and concise communications among all of the team members here, as any time wasted will only translate into further downtime, which could be detrimental in the end. Also, make sure that all contact information is up to date.

2. <u>Moving your equipment</u>: Depending upon the kind of DR setup you choose to establish (as reviewed in the last section), the DRP needs to have a component as to how all of the employee-related equipment will be moved. Although your IT infrastructure will be replicated in a cloud infrastructure or at the secondary physical site, there are still things that have to be immediately transitioned over, in order for your employees to bring your business back to a normal state of operations once again. This includes all workstations, computers, and wireless devices that are used to conduct everyday job functions. In this regard, it is also wise to make advanced plans with a moving company that specializes in DR so that items can be moved very quickly. In this regard, your DR

team should also keep an active inventory of all of these items, and make sure that it is always updated.

3. Business continuity: Another plan that must be created in conjunction with the DRP is the business continuity plan. This document or set of documents should specifically detail how the business will continue to keep running in a normal state once the mission-critical processes are back up and fully operational. By compiling this plan, you will get a solid understanding as well as to how the business truly functions and operates. As a result of this, you and your DR team will know exactly what operations and processes need to be brought up again in their order of relevant importance. Keep in mind that while the business continuity plan is actually a separate entity, the major highlights of it should be included, in the DRP.

4. Daily checks on the data backups: Although the backup databases and the confidential information and data they contain will either reside in a cloud infrastructure or at a physical off-site location, it is very important that they are tested on a regular basis to make sure that they are still working under optimal conditions and will be ready to be deployed and go into action in the aftermath of a cyberattack. Equally critical is that they are also updated with the latest software upgrades and patches and that they reflect the most recent copies of your primary databases. In other words, whatever procedures you carry out on the primary databases should also be carried out onto the backup databases, preferably on the same day, so that everything remains as current as possible and in a constant of readiness.

5. Restoring operations with the vendors: Apart from bringing back your operations to a normal state once again, it is also equally important to have a part in the DRP that outlines how you will restore communications and processes with your suppliers and vendors. The bottom line is that any downtime lost in the production of goods

and services will only result in lost customers in a very short period of time. Therefore, you will need to work out some sort of system with your external third parties in order to make sure that the needed parts, components, and supplies will be fully stocked once you are ready to resume back to a production status once again.

6. Document recovery: Apart from the intellectual property (IP) that your business may have, another key asset that your business possesses is all of the documents that it possesses. This can range anywhere from employee records to financial statements to even internal user manuals. Therefore, it is very imperative that these are backed up as well, in line with the same manner as it has been detailed with the data backups. In this scenario, you may even want to contract out this kind of service to a well-reputed document restoration company, who will be able to help your DR team to bring back all documentation online after mission-critical operations have deemed to be fully functional.

The Need for a Business Continuity Plan

There is no doubt that in today's time, the world is on edge, and there is a sense of extreme angst and confusion among businesses worldwide. True, this was probably to some degree in existence before, given the ever-changing dynamics of the cybersecurity threat landscape. But, the COVID-19 pandemic has certainly triggered this to even higher levels that were never seen before.

For example, many businesses across Corporate America were not prepared for the mass exodus that transpired with regards to working from home (aka WFH). Although nobody could have ever predicted the deep and far-reaching magnitudes of the COVID-19 pandemic, these organizations did not have a plan in place in order to make this transition into an efficient and seamless one.

The mentality always is: if my business has never been hit by a cyberattack or some other natural disaster, then why worry about it, because it will never happen to me. Well, that fundamental error in thinking will now drastically change, as many in the C-Suite, such as the CEO, CIO and/or CISO, are now starting to come to grips with the realization of the need for such a plan.

This plan is also known as the business continuity plan or BC plan in short and is the focal point of this chapter.

The Alarming Statistics of the Lack of Proper BC Planning

For those businesses that still do not yet have a solid BC plan in place, the following statistics should be an alarming factor for anybody in the C-Suite, for example:

- Typically, about 20% of organizations, on an annual basis, face some sort of either a natural disaster or a large-scale cyberattack. Of this group, 80% of those without such a plan will shut their doors permanently in just one year, if not shorter.
- 60% of the companies that succumb to a data breach will go out of business in just six months because they do not have proper mechanisms in place in order to restore the Personal Identifiable Information (PII) of their customer records after they have been impacted.
- Only 35% of the SMBs have a BC plan in place and that is ready to be implemented at a moment's notice.

Now, let us look at the financial losses because of the lack of having a BC plan:

- On average, Corporate America loses roughly a staggering $12 billion per year because they simply cannot restore the data that they have lost.

- The downtime in costs for a business to recover any lost, mission critical files is a ***whopping $5,000 per minute***.
- 80% of the SMBs that have experienced downtime due to a natural disaster or cyberattack is a ***staggering $20,000 per hour***.
- 52% of businesses in Corporate America are constantly facing numerous data backup failures per year, either because they do not have a BC plan in place, or if they have one, it is not updated on a regular basis.

Also keep in mind that natural disasters and external cyberattackers are just one part of the puzzle. The other component is those of Insider attacks, in which an employee launches threat vectors from within your IT and/or network infrastructure.

But be known, that on average, at least ***70% of all successful attacks on network-based assets*** (such as shared resources) were done by an employee of a business (Source: 1).

Now, as a member of the C-Suite, you simply cannot report these kinds of numbers to your board of directors if you have been impacted. If you do, the chances are that you will lose your job in a heartbeat, and possibly face severe financial penalties that are currently imposed by the laws of the CCPA and the GDPR.

So, what can be done so you and your business can avoid becoming one of these above-mentioned statistics? The answer is simple: Create a rock-solid BC plan, implement it, and enforce it all levels.

The Components That Go into a Business Continuity Plan

The following lists some of the key essentials that you must have in a BC plan. Keep in mind, though, that this is just a starting point for you, the CEO, CIO, and/or CISO to consider, but you must craft your plan from scratch that meets the exacting security requirements of your business:

1. <u>Determining what actually constitutes a good BC plan</u>: Before you and your employees can even embark on this process, you must first answer the following questions to help you refine the objectives and specific goals of your BC plan:
   - First, why does my business even need one if at all? This should be the easiest to answer: To restore mission-critical applications as quickly as possible.
   - What are the triggers for initiating a BC plan into action? To protect your business from all angles that could be of tremendous impact, such as natural disasters, external cyberattacks, and insider attacks.
   - What are the responsibilities of each team member of the BC team?
     No need to get into the specifics here, just a general overview is enough at this point.
   - What will the communications process be like?
     Again, just a general overview is enough, as the specifics of this will be addressed in a later section of the BC plan.
   - What is the probability of such disaster events in transpiring and what will their business impact be?
     In this situation, even before writing the BC plan, you must first conduct a risk assessment study, which is when you identify all of the assets that are both digital and physical in nature. Then from there, you need to determine which of those are most at risk, going all the way to the ones least at risk. You need to use some sort of categorization scale in this regard.
   - What technologies can be used to restore mission-critical applications in a short period of time?
     The answer to a certain degree is also pretty straightforward here. If you have on-premises IT/network infrastructure, it will take a lot longer, versus if you have a cloud-based infrastructure, such as using Microsoft Azure.

- What are the specific gaps or areas of weaknesses that need to be filled?
  The risk assessment study will reveal these to a certain degree, but in order to get the complete picture, you will also need to **_conduct a thorough penetration testing and threat hunting exercises_** to truly see where the unknown gaps and weaknesses reside at. By doing this ahead of time, that means in you are impacted, you will actually experience a shorter downtime if you are hit.
2. Ascertaining who will be doing what: This is probably one of the first detailed sections of your BC plan. At this point, you are formally deciding which employees will be doing what, as well as allocating the resources that they need to get things done quickly and efficiently. Some of the key topics that need to be spelled out here in include the following:
   - Those employees that will lead the charge in practicing the BC plan (which should be done at least on a semiannual basis) and those that will be responsible in updating it in real time after each mock scenario has been carried out. Typically, you will want your IT security staff to do this part.
   - The identification of new risks and how to mitigate them. Remember, just because you have initially addressed them in the formal risk assessment study, it does not simply stop there. As the CIO and/or CISO, you have to do this on a continual basis, so that you can stay one step ahead of the cyberattacker.
   - Once you have determined which employee will and what kinds of certain tasks and actions in the BC process, you also need to train them and keep continuing to do so on a regular basis. This section of the BC plan should exactly spell out the kinds of

training that your designated employees will receive, and frequency of when this will actually occur.

■ Communications will also be a central piece in your BC plan. You need to specify who will be the communication leaders and their roles in the time of a crisis.

■ Determining when the actual BC plan needs to be initiated. Obviously, it does not have to be activated for each and every minor security incident that occurs, but being the CIO and/or the CISO of your company, it is your call when this plan should be activated, and under conditions which this will actually happen should be spelled out here.

3. <u>The disaster recovery procedures</u>: In this part of the BC plan, you will actually be establishing the granular and minute details as to how your business plans to recover from a natural attack or cyberattack. This section should contain as much as of this detail as possible, and in fact, this is probably the one part of the BC plan that should be rehearsed and practiced.

Also, it should be kept in mind that as you establish the groundwork for this section, you also need to take into consideration if you will have a secondary, brick and mortar office from which you will transition to as the restoration takes place. This will be most likely if your business still utilizes an on-premises IT infrastructure, but if it is all based on a cloud platform, then you and your employees will be able to work from home until the damage at the physical location of your business has been mitigated.

Here are some of the steps which should be included in this subsection of the BC plan:

■ How the leads of the BC team will initiate and delegate the specific actions and steps that need to take place for the designated employees to carry out in order to fully execute the restoration process.

- How the affected computers and wireless devices will be examined for actual evidence of the security breach that occurred, and if they can be repaired or need to be replaced all together. In this part, it is highly advisable that you make use a skilled forensics expert.
- How the other stakeholders will be communicated of the events that have transpired, how they are currently being mitigated, and what is being done to bring the business back to a normal state of activities.
- In what manner the any emergency funds will be tapped into, and how it will be allocated. Being the CEO, CIO, and/or CISO, obviously your attention will be divided elsewhere, so it is very crucial that you delegate this particular responsibility to a team that you can trust, such as your accounting or finance departments.
- If you make use of a secondary site, you need to determine how your employees will be transported there, if need be. This mode of transportation should be ready to go at literally within a few hours' notice. For example, if your employees are going to be renting cars temporarily, then it is imperative that you work out some sort of contractual agreement with a car rental agency.
- If you have a cybersecurity insurance policy, it is also crucial that you file your claim as quickly as possible, as it could take some time to fully collect your payout. Remember, that filing a cybersecurity insurance claim is not exactly the same thing as filing a car or medical insurance claim. There will be many pieces put together, as your provider will most likely ask for a comprehensive report as well, including the pieces of evidence that was collected.
4. <u>The technologies that will be used</u>: Depending upon the sheer level of the magnitude of the security breach, it could be the case that your entire IT and network

infrastructures could be entirely wiped out. If your business is still using an on-premises system, you will then have to figure out ahead of time how the new computers, servers, wireless devices, as well as security tools will be procured, sent, set up, and allocated at the temporary site. The following applies to this kind of scenario, and thus, discussed in detail in this subsection of the BC plan:

■ The establishment of how the data recovery and future backup processes will be conducted at the temporary site and how this process will specifically continue once your principal location is back up and running again.

■ How your IT security team will deploy the necessary antivirus and antimalware software applications onto each and every device.

■ How your IT security team will reconfigure the new security tools and to what newer thresholds they be established so that you do not become a victim of a cyberattack yet once again at your temporary site.

■ If your business is large enough so that is has a dedicated data center or even a security operations center (aka SOC) you also need to carefully craft out in this part of the BC plan as to how you will reestablish these as well at your temporary site. For example, will new, physical locations have to be established in the interim after you have been impacted, or as the CIO and/or CISO, are you planning to fully outsource this particular function to an external third party while you at the temporary site?

But, if your entire IT and network infrastructure is in the cloud (once again, like Azure), then the transition to a temporary office location should be a pretty seamless process. Since everything will be done for you by the cloud provider, all that you have to really consider is how you will get new laptops and wireless devices to your employees so that they can access the virtual servers and virtual desktops and can conduct their daily job tasks as productively as possible.

5. The lines of communications that will take place: Along with establishing the exact restoration procedures to take place, this subsection of the BC plan is also of great importance. In sum, this section discusses in detail how the communications process will take place, so that any confusions or misunderstandings will be kept to a minimum in case you are impacted. Items to seriously consider in this subsection include the following:

   ■ The emergency communication methods: You need to determine what is the best way to contact the other members of the BC team and you also need to make sure that they will respond quickly. For example, will you reach out primarily by Email, phone, or via SMS messaging? Ideally, you should use a combination of all three modes, just to have the redundancy in case or one or even two modes of communications are not working.

   ■ The determination of the structure of the calling trees: Obviously, your BC team cannot contact everybody at once, so therefore, this is where the calling tree comes into play. In other words, you lay out a simple flow chart that can be followed quickly to determine who should contacted first, second, third, etc., in a logical, sequential fashion.

   ■ Contact information is still relevant: You need to make sure that all contact details are kept up to date with latest Email addresses and phone numbers. In this regard, you should also consider seriously setting up a separate Email address for members of the BC team so that they will notice immediately if an emergency Email has come through.

   ■ The creation of external websites and call in numbers: As far as possible, you should never use social media sites to keep the stakeholders and customers of your business updated onto the progress of how things are coming back to normal. The primary reason for this is that anything posted here can go viral in literally a matter of minutes, thus even further ruining your brand and reputation. Also, any content posted in this regard can also become a grave security concern, because the cyberattacker can quite easily hack into your social media accounts and make things even worse if they are not already.

The Need for Effective Penetration Testing

Even before the next pandemic or large-scale attacks hit, the CISO and his or her IT security team need to make sure that their walls of defenses are heavily fortified at all times and that all unknown weaknesses, gaps, and vulnerabilities are identified and fully mitigated.

For example, when COVID-19 hit, many businesses in Corporate America had many backdoors that were still left wide open, as well as many gaps. Because of this, the cyberattacker was able to take full and complete advantage of this and fully expose these weaknesses at the height of the pandemic. Therefore, the need for penetration testing is very much needed. This can be considered as a deep dive test into the IT and network infrastructure of any business.

With this type of exercises being conducted, your defense perimeters will be examined in great detail from both the internal environment and the external environment. It is only through this kind of exhaustive testing that ***all hidden vulnerabilities, weaknesses, and holes will be unearthed***.

In other words, a penetration testing team will literally break down the walls of defenses at your business, using real-world threat variants that a cyberattacker would use. But of course, this is all done ethically and legally, per the contracts that you have signed with them. At the end of the testing cycles, a comprehensive report will be prepared for you as to the unknown vulnerabilities that were discovered, as well as the steps that you can take to correct and remediate them.

In this article, we take a look at the different kinds of teams that are involved and what their specific duties are. They are broken down into the following three different categories:

- The red team;
- The blue team;
- The purple team.

The Red Team

It is the red team that has the primary responsibility of launching an "ethical-based" cyberattack against the defense perimeters of your business. But it is important to note here that the red team is not particularly interested in what is being attacked, ***they are much more interested instead on the access methods to get to those targets***.

The red team will use a large amount of creativity and even use techniques one many never even have heard of. Remember, the goal of the red team is to not just attack your lines of defense but breach them through each and every means that are available at their disposal. To do this, they will think and act just like a real cyberattacker, but very often come up with ideas on their own as well.

When a red team engages in its mock cyberattacks, they very often do not ask for a specific list of targets to hit. Rather, they are also interested in those systems in your IT infrastructure that are "out of scope". As a result, this gives the red team a much broader set of permutations to examine. Because of this, the red team will " ... find vulnerabilities that stem from cultural bias in system design, flawed conclusions, or the limitations and expectations of an insider perspective" (Source: 5).

It is important to note that red teams often make use of a methodology known as the "Layered Approach". With this, multiple attempts are utilized in order to break through the lines of defense at the business entity. These attempts are not done successively, rather they are done simultaneously, in order to cause the highest levels of confusion and mayhem for the blue team.

For example, one part of the red team may try to hack into the password database, while at the same time, another part of the red team could try to gain access to the main entry of the organization by using covertly replicated access cards.

It is important to note that effective red team testing just does not happen over a short period of time. It can take up to a year to examine what to hit, as a real cyberattacker these days will take their own time as well in determining and researching their targets.

A primary advantage of having a red team conduct your penetration testing is that they will offer an unbiased, holistic view of the weaknesses not only in your IT infrastructure, but also among your employees and the physical conditions of your office location(s).

The Blue Team

The overall, arching task of the blue team is fight off the cyberattack that has been launched by the red team. They will also work in conjunction with your existing IT security team in this regard. But apart from this, the blue team has other specific responsibilities in the efforts to overcome the cyberattack. These are as follows:

1. Preparedness: The blue team will do everything possible in its role in order to protect the business or corporation from any looming cyber-based threats. This will include testing of all of the security technologies that are in place in order to make sure that they are in optimized to

detect any sort of anomalies or outliers; making sure that the incident response and the DRPs are set in motion should a cyberattack actually occur; ***keeping all employees informed*** of the upcoming cyber threat landscape.

2. <u>Identification</u>: Here, the blue team will make every effort to correctly identify any potential cyberattacks that are posed to the business or corporation.

3. <u>Containment</u>: If the organization is hit by a cyberattack, it will then become the responsibility of the blue team to contain the damage caused by the attack in this regard, one of the best tools that the blue team will have at hand is the incident response plan. By initiating at the time of the cyberattack, the members of the incident response team will also be called into action in order to mitigate any losses from the cyberattack.

4. <u>Recovery</u>: In the unfortunate chance that the business or corporation has been breached by a cyberattack, it will also be one of the main responsibilities of the blue team to also activate the DRPs in order to bring the entity back at a predefined level of operations before the incident occurred. This should occur, at maximum, no more than one or two days after the cyberattack. At this point, one of the main priorities of the blue team is to bring up many mission-critical processes as possible during this short time span.

5. <u>Lessons learned</u>: Obviously, once the damage from the cyberattack has been mitigated, and the organization is up and running at near 100% operational levels, a forensics investigation team will be called in to conduct an exhaustive study as to what happened and how the cyberattack could have been avoided. It is also one of the responsibilities of the blue team to compile all of this into a report, as well as to formulate strategies as to how such types of incidents can be avoided in the future.

The blue team during the penetration testing exercise(s) also assumes the following responsibilities:

1. <u>Operation system hardening</u>: The blue team will further fortify the operating systems of all of the hardware that is being used at the business or corporation. This will include primarily all of the servers, workstations, and wireless devices (securing both the Android and iOS). The goal here is to decrease the "surface of vulnerability" of all the operating systems that are currently being used.
2. <u>The perimeter defense</u>: The blue team will also ensure that all firewalls, network intrusion devices, routers, traffic flow devices, packet filtering devices, etc., are all up and running, and operating at peak conditions.

In order to further fend off any cyberattacks, the blue team typically uses such tools as log management and analysis, and SIEM technology.

The Purple Team

The primary objective of the purple team is to maximize the capabilities of both the red team and the blue team. For example, with the former, the purple team can "… evaluate your security controls and ability to detect attacks, compromise, lateral movement, command and control communications, and data exfiltration" (Source: 6).

In other words, after the red team has evaluated what kind of cyberattacks they are going to launch toward your lines of defense, the purple team can also further enhance these efforts by brainstorming newer kinds of cyber threats that can be launched, as well as new attack vectors.

In turn, the purple team can also work hand in hand with the blue team in order to make sure that they have followed the steps for cyberattack preparedness. In this regard, the purple team can also conduct a comprehensive audit check to make sure that the blue team has not left anything out in their preparation processes.

In fact, the purple team should be viewed as a "Neutral Party" when a penetration testing exercise(s) is carried out. In other words, they do not attack or defend, they actually do both, and lend a hand to both sides of the equation, by sharing intelligence. Different members of the red team and the blue team will take their own corresponding turns on participating in the purple team. In this regard, the size of the purple team should be kept relatively small – perhaps no more than two members from either the red team or the blue team. But, in the end, it is not the size of the team matters, it is the level and the breadth of the team member's experience that matters the most.

Some of the primary objectives of a purple team include the following:

1. Working with both the red team and blue team in a harmonious fashion: This includes making observations and notes as to how the two teams are working together, and making any recommendations to change the team compositions, or to make any needed adjustments to the penetration exercise(s) themselves.
2. Understanding and visualizing the big picture: This means assuming the frame mind, thinking processes, and the responsibilities of both the red team and the blue team.
3. Assuming an overall responsibility for the penetration testing exercise(s): This simply refers to analyzing and interpreting results to the client and taking and remedial or corrective actions that are needed. For example, this could include coming up with a schedule for downloading and implementing software patches and upgrades, providing recommendations to improve security awareness training for the employees of the organization that is being penetration tested.
4. Delivering the maximum value to the client: By collecting information and data from both the red team and the

blue team, the purple team can, as stated before, deliver a high-quality document to the client, with the end result being that the lines of defenses will only be that much more fortified.

The Different Types of Penetration Testing

The last section of this chapter discusses the sheer importance of penetration testing and what is done by the various teams. But, there are different types of penetration testing that can be done, depending upon the requirements of the business, so that they will not become a victim during the next round of a COVID-19 pandemic.

The External Penetration Test

What Is It?

When people talk about penetration testing, they often confuse the internal kind with the external one. However, there are key differences between the two. For example, with the former, the pen testing team is looking for vulnerabilities that may lie from within the internal environment of your business. This typically includes the following:

■ Access points (these can include both logical and physical based);
■ The Wi-Fi system;
■ Firewalls, routers, and network intrusion devices.

But with the latter, the following are examined to ascertain the weaknesses that could potentially exist from the outside environment of your business. In other words, you want to find out where those undiscovered gaps if a cyberattacker were to attack your lines of defense from the outside going in (after all, that is their primary objective in the end).

The testing here typically includes the following:

■ Source code testing (especially those of web-based applications);
■ Identity management testing;
■ Authentication/authorization testing;
■ The testing of any other types of client facing applications (this is now becoming very crucial, especially as the remote workforce now starts to take a permanent hold);
■ The testing of the integrity of the lines of network communications, especially taking a very careful examination of the virtual private networks (VPNs) that are currently being used;
■ The testing of the various session management systems that are taking place between the server and the client, as you do not want network-based requests to go unfulfilled for an extensive period of time;
■ The testing and examination of any encryption-based systems that are deployed along your lines of defense.

The Stages of External Penetration Testing

It is important to keep in mind that conducting this kind of test simply does not just involve putting a red team (these are the ethical hackers that try to penetrate your business from the external environment) and simply throwing everything that they have at their disposal against your digital assets. Rather, a methodological approach needs to be taken, and the following are the major components of it:

1. <u>The planning and reconnaissance phase</u>: Shortly after all the contracts and legal agreements have been signed

between the company doing the actual pen test and the client, this is the first step that needs to be accomplished. With this, the red team will take time and prioritize what needs to be done first. For example, they will attempt gain a comprehensive understanding of those types of threat variants that your business is most prone to, by carefully studying the risk assessment analysis that you initially conducted. From here, the red team can target the most vulnerable digital assets first. Apart from this, they can also conduct various online testing exercises to pinpoint other facets which need to be examined, such as those items that did not appear in the analysis. This phase can be deemed to be the information gathering session, so that the red team can get a detailed, holistic view of what your entire IT and network infrastructure looks like.

2. <u>The scanning of the targets</u>: This is the stage where the red team will take the mindset of a real-world cyberattacker with a nefarious intent and start to hit upon those targets which appear to offer the most prized possessions that can be yielded. This includes items such as confidential company documents, IP, the PII datasets of both your customers and employees (typically this will be credit card numbers, social security numbers, usernames/passwords, and other sorts of banking/financial information), etc. Some examples of the targets in this aspect include the following:

   ■ Servers which contain shared resources;
   ■ Databases which house the mission critical information/data;
   ■ The identification of any shared or open parts that exist in your network infrastructure;
   ■ The location of FTP servers (because usernames and passwords are usually entered in as cleartext here);
   ■ Any email servers;

- ■ The location of any outdated or weak SSL certificates in an effort to deploy malicious payloads that can be used, for example, in a SQL injection attack.
3. The gaining and maintaining of access: Once the weak spots have been determined from the second step, the next phase is to attempt to gain access into them and maintain it for as long as possible. This is usually done by finding and locating those backdoors that were not known of before. It is important to keep in mind that the cyberattacker is not going to just find one way in. They will try to find all possible avenues, so they can use a combination of them at infrequent intervals in order to go undiscovered.
4. The exploitation: Once the red team has gained access to what they have laid down the objectives for, the final step in the exercise is to now try to further exploit all the weaknesses, gaps, and vulnerabilities that have been discovered and steal the proverbial "Crown Jewels". One thing that should be noted here is that the red team will try to stay as long as possible into whatever they have penetrated, and to launch the exfiltration process in a slow fashion, bit by bit at a time. The goal of this is to avoid the detection by the internal network systems, by not giving out any kind of abnormal behavioral signatures, which can happen if the "Crown Jewels" were being taken out in bigger chunks.

What Is Web Application Testing?

In today's digital world, everything is pretty much made available in the Internet. Because of this, the demand for robust and effective web-based applications remains strong, and will continue to be so, for a very long time to come.

A major catalyst for this has been the advent with remote workforce, with about all employees using web interfaces to get their daily job tasks done.

Thus, the need to critically test web applications before they are deployed into the production environment is now greater than ever before. This is where the role of penetration testing comes into play. Put in simple terms, the goal of conducting these kinds of exercises is to see where all of the vulnerabilities, weaknesses, and gaps reside in them. Once all of these have been assessed, remediative actions are then provided so that they will not be an issue once the actual product has been sent to the client.

This kind of testing is normally quite exhaustive in nature and typically involves checking for the following:

- Overall functionality;
- Built in functionality;
- Databases.

The next section provides a more detailed overview of these.

The Components of Web App Penetration Testing

Although the depth and the scope of the exact penetration test (aka "Pen Test") to be executed is primarily dependent upon the needs of the client, to varying degrees, they typically include the following:

1) The testing for overall functionality: This involves testing for different items such as the GUI interface, the APIs that are being used (especially if they are open sourced in nature); the databases that will be populated with confidential information and data [this includes the PII datasets]; and other financial data that will be stored in them by the customer; and testing the web application

from both the server side (which involves testing the server upon which the web application is hosted) and the client side (this is the interface that the end user will interact with on a day to day basis).

2) <u>The testing for built-in functionality</u>: This kind of examination usually looks at seeing how the individual components of the web application work together in a holistic fashion, and the following is usually tested the most:

- The testing of all links. This includes the outbound links; internal links; any "mail to" links; as well as anchor links.

- The checking of forms. This mostly involves the "Contact Us" page, but it can include others as well, such as the ones used for lead generation purposes. In this regard, all of the scripts must be checked (for example, most of these are written in PHP, Perl, etc.); any default fields populated should be correct; numerical values; confirming that the right information/data that are entered in by the end user are being transmitted and stored into the database(s); making sure that the UI/UX environment is compatible to all platforms (such as that of the Android and the iOS) and all devices (like notebooks, tablets, smartphones, etc.). Also, given the ramifications of both the GDPR and the CCPA, you also need to make sure that the appropriate verbiage exists on the web application stating that the end user agrees to having their information stored, and if not, how they can opt out of it.

- The testing of cookies. This procedure involves making sure that they are appropriately deleted or expire when they are supposed to.

- The testing of both the HTML and the CSS. This is probably one of the most critical aspects. Although other different web application programming languages can be used in lieu of HTML, the bottom line is that the code used to create the web application must be tested inside and out, especially when it comes to the usage of APIs. If this is not done, there are backdoors that can be left behind, thus leaving a gaping point of entry for the cyberattacker.

■ The examination of compliance requirements. With data privacy now becoming a hot button topic very much, you need to pen test the source code so that is not only compliant with the GDPR and the CCPA, but also with the various NIST and ISO standards, but also those that have been set forth by the W3C.

3) <u>The testing of the database functionality</u>: Although this kind of test addressed overall functionality, it is still extremely important to test the database(s) that will be connected to the web application. Whatever tool is used to create them (such as SQL Server, MySQL, etc.), the following must be examined:

■ The examination of any errors that may come up as result of executing any type or kind of query. This can be accomplished by making use of test datasets.

■ Confirming that any data or information that is transmitted to and from the end user and web application remains intact and stays that way after it is stored in the database. Equally important here is making sure that the layers of encryption that have been deployed are strong enough are not difficult to break through.

■ Making sure that the responses for any queries are handled in an optimal way and are done within a well-established time limit. It is important to keep in mind that if the response time is too long, this can literally "hang up" the web application and could pose a serious security vulnerability.

Understanding the Importance of the VAPT

In the world of cybersecurity today, there is one thing that is plenty of: tests and examinations to make sure that the lines of defenses surrounding your business are well fortified. Typically, it is both your internal and external environment that are critically assessed. Overall, one of the primary goals of conducting these exercises is to determine where both the known and the unknown weaknesses are and to formulate the right strategy so that they can be remediated quickly and effectively.

One such test is known as the "VAPT" and is the focal point article.

The Components

VAPT is an acronym that stands for "Vulnerability Assessment and Penetration Testing". As its name implies, there are two parts to it, which are as follows:

1. The vulnerability assessment: This is the process where the needed tests are conducted in order to determine where the backdoors exist in a particular software application that your company has developed, or within a certain part of your network segment, which is typically known as a "Subnet". It is important to keep in mind that this kind of exercise is ***not designed to examine your entire IT and network infrastructure***, as there are other kinds of tests that can take that holistic type of approach.

2. The penetration test: This is a more familiar term to most people, and this is the type of approach that is used to unearth those weaknesses that reside in your application or Subnet. However, depending upon your other security requirements, a penetration test can also be used to examine all of the digital assets in your company.

The Causes for the Vulnerabilities to Exist

One of the common questions that are often asked is why are there vulnerabilities in the apps in the first place? Some of the common reasons include the following:

■ Poor software development: Very often, the testing of the source code is often left to the very end of the project, even if it is done at all. Due to the crunch to deliver the final project to the client, the time that is needed to discover any holes in the source code is often not allocated. Also many software development teams make use of third-party APIs (which are open sourced based) and in this regard, these software libraries are falsely assumed to be safe to use and are not tested to the unique environment that is being used to create the software application.

■ Misconfigurations: With the advent of a near 99% remote workforce that is transpiring today, many companies are now opting to move their entire on-premises infrastructure to a cloud-based platform, such as that of the AWS or Microsoft Azure. Even though these provide much more secure environments, new vulnerabilities crop up in the virtualized IT/network infrastructure because of particular settings not being configured properly. The fallacy in thinking is that the settings that worked On Prem will also work in the exact same way for the cloud-based environment. As a result, making sure that all of the settings have been established after the migration to the cloud becomes an ignored task.

■ Weak passwords: Even though many businesses have implemented two-factor authentication ("2FA"), and are moving cautiously toward the Zero Trust Framework, the use of weak passwords still very much persists. Because of that, they are also a root cause of app and Subnet vulnerabilities. For example, even though password managers are now widely used to create hard to break passwords, humans, by nature, are still creatures of habit. In other words, we still want to use the same, very easy to remember password, and use the same one when it comes to accessing shared resources on the servers.

The Types of Vulnerability Testing

From within the VAPT framework, there are number of key exercises that can be performed, and in general, they typically include the following:

1. Active testing: This is where the tester will actually examine the software application or Subnet in a real time basis, by using some sort of test data. As the tests are being done and the results are reported back, remediations will also be formulated on the spot and sent back to the client. The goal of this fixes up any vulnerabilities, gaps, or weaknesses in the shortest period of time possible, so that there are no further risks that are posed.
2. Passive testing: In this regard, the tester is simply running a rudimentary scan, and there is no test data that is implemented. In other words, whatever gaps show up as a result are collected into one report, and from there, remediative actions are then provided to the client.
3. Network testing: With this type of scan, the tester will carefully examine the current state of configurations in the Subnet and will compare that against a list of what should be established. The purpose of this approach is to paint a clear picture of those network thresholds that need to reset, in the shortest time possible, so that there are no further risks posed to their cloud-based infrastructure.
4. Distributed testing: As mentioned previously in the VAPT model, only one software application or Subnet is typically examined. But if those instances arise where

multiple apps have to be tested at the same time, then the scans can be modified to accommodate, via the use of "Distributed Testing".

Dark Web Monitoring

Using the Internet today is second nature to most us. We take it for granted on a daily basis. But however, when something goes wrong with it, or it simply is not there for a short period of time, a feeling of paralysis very often sets in. But what we use today for searching, communications, and even purchasing goods and services is just one part of the Internet.

In fact, this is known as the "Clear Web" or the "Indexed Web". This portion is what is available to the public, and at the present time, there are well over 6,000,000,000 websites that are currently visible, or "indexed". Even though this may seem like a huge amount, it accounts for only about 1%–4% of the total Internet. The other remaining 96% is not available to the public, and thus is known as the "Dark Web" (Source: 7).

What Is the Dark Web?

The dark web is very often thought of the place where underground criminal and illicit activities take place. While this is for the most part true, the dark web is also used for legal purposes, there are times that this is not the case. The dark web can only be accessed via a special web browser which is known as "Tor".

It cannot be accessed by the current browsers such as Microsoft Edge, Google Chrome, or the iOS Safari. But when it comes to cybersecurity, the dark web is often the place where the cyberattacker will come to first in order to procure services in which they can launch their threat variants.

But typically these days, it is the dark web also where the cyberattacker can unload all of the crown jewels that they have seized from launching a covert attack. This very often includes usernames/passwords, credit card numbers, social security numbers, patient health data, financial or other kinds of banking information, etc.

The primary goal here is to sell all of this for a rather handsome profit. Therefore, along with other protective measures that a company may take (which will of course include penetration testing), routinely scanning the dark web to see if any PII datasets (such as those that are associated with your employees and customers) have been dumped here is just as important as well.

This is technically known as "Dark Web Monitoring".

The Importance and Benefits of It

It is important to note at this point that the terms "Dark Web Monitoring" and "Dark Web Scanning" are very often used synonymously. However, the two are very different in their meaning. The former refers to monitoring the dark web on a regular and frequent basis, whereas the latter refers to doing just a one-off dive into the dark web. In order to keep your company well protected, it is therefore highly recommended that your IT security team engage in the active and frequent monitoring of it.

There is also confusion about whether dark web monitoring also involves penetration testing. Truth be told, it does not. The primary reason for this is that there are many parts of it that are still sealed off, and when you do a deep dive into it, you want to keep your identity secret as much as possible. Also, keep in mind that penetration testing can often take quite some time to accomplish, and when you are in the dark web, you want to stay for as little as possible so that your IT security team cannot be tracked down.

Therefore, the primary activities that you will be engaged in for the most part will be visiting and monitoring the various forums and online stores where any heisted PII datasets are often bought and sold at.

The Benefits

There are other benefits to conducting dark web monitoring exercises, and these include the following:

1. <u>Cutting down on any further damage</u>: The trend today is for the cyberattacker to take a long time to study the profiles of their intended victims. They do this in order to determine the most vulnerable point in which they can penetrate covertly. Once in, the goal is to stay in for as long as possible and moving in a lateral fashion so that other areas of the IT/network infrastructure can be entered into as well. The PII datasets are not going to be stolen in one huge swipe; rather, they will be taken out bit by bit so that your IT security team does not notice it, until is too late. But if you engage in routine monitoring of the dark web, and if by chance you come across any information/data that looks like were stolen from your company; this will be your first indication that a cyberattacker has entered into your system. From here, you can then take the actions to kick them out of your IT/network infrastructure, and seal off any holes that are still lurking (this is where a penetration test can be used in conjunction with the dark web monitoring exercise). Of course, the sooner you do this, the better, before the real damage starts to set in for your company.
2. <u>You can beef up your lines of defenses</u>: The common thinking here is that by merely conducting a cyber risk analysis you will then know exactly the steps that you need to take make your defense perimeter even stronger.

While this is certainly true to an extent, engaging in dark web monitoring can also help you to further pinpoint those areas in defense mechanisms that still need more work. For example, once you know that some of your PII datasets have actually found their way onto the dark web, your IT security team can then backtrack to determine the manner in which how they were actually stolen. From there, you will then be able to determine where the weak spot was. For example, even though your databases may have been upgraded with the latest patches and upgrades, there could have been a security flaw in the source code which allowed the cyberattacker to penetrate into and covertly hijack this information.

3. Coming into compliance: With advent of the remote workforce now taking a permanent hold, it is highly expected that both the GDPR and the CCPA will now be strictly enforced. A major part of these key pieces of legislation is making sure that the PII datasets that are housed in your database are protected by the best layers of defense possible. By demonstrating to regulators, you can prove to them that you are taking a proactive stance in taking further steps to protect these mission critical pieces of information and data, if you are ever audited. Also, by engaging in this kind of activity now, you will be able to quickly implement the right controls which are needed in case your IT security team has discovered any corporate information/data for sale on the dark web before it is too late.

The Differences between a Vulnerability Assessment and a Penetration Test

Although one of the previous subsections of this chapter described how a vulnerability assessment and penetration test can work together, there are major differences between the two and they are detailed in this subsection of this chapter.

Breaking Down What Vulnerability Scanning and Penetration Testing Are

In the world of cybersecurity, there are many ways to find out where the strengths and weaknesses lie in your lines of defense. One method is conducting a risk assessment. With this, you are tallying up a list of all of your digital assets, and based upon the controls that they have, you are ranking them on a categorical scale of how vulnerable they are to a security breach.

Although this is an effective method, it is based heavily on human intuition, so there could be a lot of subjectivity involved.

There are other tests which will give you a much accurate look into this level of vulnerability, without any biases incurred. These are known as vulnerability scans and penetration testing. While these two are used interchangeably with another, they are actually quite different methodologies, which will be further explored in this article.

Vulnerability Assessments

This type of test runs automated scans across the major components that reside in both your IT and network infrastructures. These primarily include the servers, and other workstations and wireless devices. These assessments primarily look for known vulnerabilities that exist, without any human intervention involved.

The scans can run as short as a few minutes to as long as a few hours. After the probing has been completed, a report is usually generated for the client, and from there, it is up to them to decide how to proceed with any specific actions to remediate the issues.

This test is also known as a "Passive" kind of test in the sense that it only detects those weaknesses that are highly visible and can be exploited very easily by a cyberattacker. This just serves as a tipping point of what other vulnerabilities could be lurking. In a sense, the vulnerability scan can be viewed as merely conducting an EKG as to what is going on in terms of risk exposure.

One of the primary advantages of this kind of assessment is the cost. It is very affordable, even to the SMB which makes it a very attractive option. The downside is that if there are any recommendations that are provided in the report, it will not be specific to your business, rather, it will just be general in nature, based upon previous threat profiles. Because of its low cost, a vulnerability scan can be run on a continual cycle, at different timing intervals.

Further, the vulnerabilities that have been discovered are not exploited to see what the root cause of these are or to see if there are other vulnerabilities that could lie underneath.

Penetration Testing

This can be viewed as the "Angiogram" in the detection of the vulnerabilities, weaknesses, and gaps that reside in your IT/network infrastructures. A huge deep dive is done, with many kinds of tests being conducted. They won't last for just a matter of a few hours, rather, they go on for long and extended periods of time.

Second, there is not much automation that is involved when conducting a penetration test. It is primarily a manual-based process, which takes the work of many skilled professionals, with years of experience. These people are also known as "Ethical Hackers" because they are taking the mindset of cyberattacker and using every tactic in the book in order to break down your walls of defense.

With this effort, these individuals are not only looking for the known vulnerabilities, but they are also looking for the __*unknown ones*__, such as covert backdoors that could have been left behind in source code development. In other words, heavy active scanning is involved, unlike the vulnerability assessments.

Third, penetration testing is not just done on digital assets. It can also be used to unearth any gaps or weaknesses that are found within the physical infrastructure of a business. For example, a team can be specifically assigned to see how easy it is replicate an ID badge and use that fool the security guard at the main point of entry.

Fourth, penetration testing can also be used to ascertain the level of vulnerability the employees have to a Social Engineering Attack. In this regard, a specialized team can be called upon to make robocalls to the finance and accounting departments to see if they can be tricked into making payments on fake invoices. Or the calls could involve reaching out to the administrative assistants of the C-Suite and luring them into wire large sums of money to a phony, offshore account.

Fifth, penetration testing can be used in both the internal and external environments of a business.

Typically, the following are the two teams involved (perhaps even three) when conducting these kinds of tests:

- The red team: These are the ethical hackers that are trying to break into your systems as previously described;
- The blue team: These are the ethical hackers that work internally with your IT security team, to see how well they react to and fend off the attacks that are being launched toward them by the red team;
- The purple team: This may or may not be used, depending upon the security requirements of the client. This team is a combination of the red and blue ones and provides an unbiased feedback to both teams as to how they have done during the course of the exercise.

At the end, the client is given an exhaustive report of the findings from the penetration test, as well as suggestions of actions that can be taken to remediate the problem. Although the biggest advantage of this kind of exercise is the deep level of thoroughness that is involved, the downside is that they can be quite expensive. As a result, penetration tests are typically only carried out perhaps once, or at most, twice a year.

Key Takeaways

The following matrix summarizes some of the key differences between a vulnerability scan and a penetration test:

Vulnerability Assessment	Penetration Test
Tests are passive	Tests are active
Tests are automated, no human intervention	Tests are primarily manual, lots of human intervention
Tests are short in time frame	Tests are much longer in time frame
Reports are provided to the client, but not specifically for actions that can remediate issues	Reports are provided to the client, and are specific to actions that remediate specific issues
Scans can be run on a continual cycle	Scanning is done only at a point in time intervals due to their exhaustive nature
Tests are primarily done on digital assets	Tests are done on both physical and digital assets
Only known vulnerabilities are discovered	Both known and unknown vulnerabilities are discovered
Costs are affordable	Costs can be quite expensive
Only general tests are done	All kinds of tests are done, depending upon the requirements of the client

The question we often get asked: "What kind of test should I get"? It all comes down to cost. Typically, the smaller businesses can only afford the vulnerability scan, whereas the medium-sized business can afford the penetration test. But truthfully, each and every business should know all of the vulnerabilities that lurk in their systems, especially the unknown ones, as this is what the cyberattacker will primarily go after.

A security breach can cost easily 10X more than any of these tests just described. Therefore, the CISO and his or her IT security team need to remain constantly proactive; thus making the penetration test the top choice to go with in the end.

The Importance of Threat Hunting

Just as important as penetration testing, so is the need for effective threat hunting. This is where the CISO and his or her IT security team are conducting deep dive tests from within the IT and network infrastructure of their business. The idea here is to find those malicious cyberattackers that are already lurking, and will take full advantage of a situation once it is ripe, such as the next COVID-19 pandemic wave.

This is reviewed in more detail in this subsection of this chapter.

What Is Threat Hunting?

There is very often a fallacy in the world of cybersecurity that simply implementing various types and kinds of security technologies toward the lines of defenses of a business or a corporation will mean greater levels of protection.

While in theory this may be true, but reality often dictates the opposite of this. For example, by simply deploying various security tools, you are actually increasing the attack surface for the cyberattacker.

For example, a CIO or a CISO may think that deploying ten firewalls is better than just having one in place. But with this thinking, they have given the cyberattacker nine more avenues in which to attack the vulnerabilities and weaknesses of the IT infrastructure.

Instead, it is far better to spend the critical financial resources for perhaps just two firewalls, ***making sure that they are strategically placed, they are needed the most will have the greatest effect***.

This kind of mindset of determining where security assets need to be placed is actually a very proactive one. The primary reason for this is that the CIO/CSIO and their IT security staff are actually taking the time to discover what areas are most at risk in their organization, what tools will be most effective and where, rather than spending money in a haphazard fashion.

In fact, this proactive way of thinking needs to be extended to the world of threat hunting as well. With this, the IT security staff are using various kinds of methodologies and tools in order to scope out and mitigate the risks of any cyberthreats that are lurking from within their IT infrastructure.

But being successful at doing this on a daily basis requires that the CIO/CISO and their IT security staff have to go above and beyond the proverbial "extra mile". How this can be achieved is reviewed in this article.

A Formal Definition of Proactive Threat Hunting

A formal definition of proactive based threat hunting is as follows:

> [It] is the process of proactively searching through networks or datasets to detect and respond to advanced cyberthreats that evade traditional rule- or signature-based security controls. Threat hunting

combines the use of threat intelligence, analytics, and automated security tools with human intelligence, experience and skills.

(Source: 8.)

In other words, there are two sub components of this definition:

1. Being proactive in any type of threat hunting exercise means that the CIO/CISO has to break away from the conventional ways of thinking, and have the ability to "think out of the box". For instance, what works in one situation more than likely will not work in another, because the cyberthreat landscape is changing on a very dynamic basis.

(Source: 8.)

2. Being proactive simply doesn't involve the use of the latest and most sophisticated of threat hunting tools. Rather, it takes not only that, but also the use of reliable information and data as well as deep motivational levels, experience, and technical know-how from the IT security staff.

Despite the importance of threat hunting in cybersecurity today, not too many businesses and corporations are implementing it, which is pointed by these stats in a recent survey in which 306 organizations were polled:

■ Only 27% of the respondents actually had a well-defined threat hunting methodology and were actually utilizing it;
■ Only 45% of the respondents had a formal plan in place in order to launch and execute a specific threat hunting exercise.

(Source: 9.)

Other stats:

- 88% of businesses feel that their existing threat hunting approaches need to be greatly improved;
- 56% of organizations feel that conducting a threat hunting exercise with their own resources (or "in-house") takes too long and consumes resources from carrying out other IT security-related duties;
- 53% of organizations feel that their threat hunting methodologies and activities are actually "tipping off" cyberattackers.

(Source: 10.)

Why are businesses and corporations not taking a proactive approach to threat hunting? The following reasons are cited:

1. The use of different tools can make threat hunting a very time-consuming proposition;
2. The collection of information and data can be a very labor-intensive process which requires third part involvement and verification;
3. There is not enough time to conduct proactive based threat hunting exercises because the IT security staff has to respond to so many false alarms that are sounded off on a daily basis;
4. Because of the enormous time constraints that are involved, only about 1% of all security alerts are actually probed into and further examined (Source: 4.);
5. Threat hunting can be a huge financial drain;
6. Threat hunting requires a very special kind of mindset – recruiting candidates for this specific talent can be very difficult.

Despite these above-mentioned obstacles, proactive threat hunting is still a much-needed function for every business and corporation, and is a process that can be achieved.

The Process of Proactive Threat Hunting and Its Components

Proactive threat hunting differs greatly from businesses to corporations, as to what needs to be specifically tracked down and mitigated depends largely upon their security environment as well as their specific requirements. But in general terms, there are four major proactive threat hunting categories, which are as follows:

1. <u>The hypothesis driven investigation</u>: This is where it is discovered that a brand-new threat vector is imminent, based upon a rather significant of information and data that is collected from the various Intelligence Feeds. Based upon this, the threat hunting team will then probe deeper into the network logs and attempt to find any hidden anomalies or trends that could be foretelling of a cyber-attack.
2. <u>The indicators of compromise (IOC) investigation</u>: This is when the threat hunting team does a "deep dive investigation" into the IT infrastructure to determine where the malicious activity is specifically taking place at, based upon the alerts and the warnings that they have received.
3. <u>The analytics-driven investigation</u>: This is where the threat hunting teams conduct targeted exercises based upon the information and the data that are collected from machine learning (ML), artificial intelligence (AI) tools.
4. <u>The TTP investigation</u>: TTP stands for tactics, techniques, and procedures threat hunting. This kind of threat hunting reveals the mannerisms in which a cyberattacker operates in. It is important to keep in mind that the cyberattacker will not use the same toolset when launching another attack; but rather, they will typically utilize the same operational techniques. This is a hierarchical threat hunting technique.

Being proactive simply doesn't involve the use of the latest and most sophisticated of threat hunting tools. Rather, it takes not only that, but also the use of reliable information and data as well as deep motivational levels, experience, and technical know-how from the IT security staff.

The Need for Endpoint Security

Even after the first wave of the COVID-19 pandemic, and with the emergence of the near 99% remote workforce, many businesses are still only concerned with securing the network lines of communications, and not the point of origination and point destination. Thus, these have become neglected areas which the cyberattacker is now taking full advantage of.

In this subsection of this chapter, we will examine just how critical this area is, especially when the next disaster strikes.

There is no doubt that the cybersecurity threat landscape is changing on a daily basis. It seems like that hardly one type of attack comes out, new variants of it are launched at a subsequent point in time. There is no doubt that it is difficult to keep up with this cat and mouse game, literally giving the IT staff of any organization a serious run for their money.

Remember, the cyberattacker of today is no rush to launch their threat vectors. As opposed from their "smash and grab" style from some time ago, they are now taking their time to select, profile, and carefully study their potential victims. This is done in an effort to find any unknown vulnerabilities and weaknesses, so that they can stay for much longer periods in the confines of their victim.

Then, once they are in, they can then accomplish their specific objectives, bit by bit, unbeknownst to their victim, until it is too late. But very often, businesses and corporations only think of protecting of what lies within their IT Infrastructure. For example, this includes the servers, the workstations, the network connections, wireless devices, etc.

The Importance for Endpoint Security

Very often, little attention is paid to fortifying the lines of defense of the endpoints of these systems. For instance, a CIO or a CISO is probably more concerned with securing the lines of network communications by using a VPN, rather than the starting and ending points of it. In this aspect, the cyber-attacker is well aware of this, and is starting to take full advantage of it in order get in and stay in forever long as they can.

Thus, as one can see, securing the endpoints of an IT Infrastructure is thus becoming of paramount importance. In this blog, we examine some of the latest, best practices that an organization can take to further enhance their endpoint security.

The Best Practices

Here is what is recommended:

1. <u>Make use of automated patching software</u>: One of the first cardinal rules of security in general is to have your IT staff to stay on top of the latest software upgrades and patches. In fact, there will be some experts that will claim that you should even have a dedicated individual to handle this particular task. Perhaps if your organization is an SMB, this could be possible. But even then, this can be quite a laborious and time-consuming process. But what about those much larger entities that perhaps have multiple IT environments and thousands of work-stations and servers? Obviously, the number of endpoints that you will have to fortify can multiply very quickly. Thus, it is highly recommended that you have a process is place that can automatically look for the relevant patches and upgrades, as well as download and deploy them.

2. <u>Have a well-trained and very proactive cyber response team</u>: Once your organization has been impacted by a cyberattack, there is no time to waste. Every minute and second that is lost just delays your recovery that much more. Therefore, you need to have a dedicated cyber response team whose primary function is to respond and mitigate the impacts of a cyberattack within a 48-hour time span, at the very maximum. In order to do this, they must be well trained, and practice on a regular basis (at least once twice a month) to real world scenarios. They also must be equipped with the latest security tools to determine if there are any other security weaknesses or vulnerabilities that have not been discovered as yet. This primarily involves finding and ascertaining any malicious behavior or abnormal trends that are occurring from within the IT Infrastructure. Also, the cyber response team needs to have a dynamic alert and warning system in place in order to notify of them any potential security breaches, especially at the endpoints.

3. <u>Perform routine security scans on your endpoints</u>: Just as important it is to maintain a routine schedule for keeping up to date with software upgrades and patches, the same holds true as well for examining the state of the endpoints in your IT Infrastructure. In fact, it should be the duty for the network administrator to formulate such a schedule, and this should include conducting exhaustive checks for any signs of potential malware. Sophisticated antivirus software needs to be deployed at the endpoints and maintained regularly. As a rule of thumb, it is recommended that these endpoint security Scans should be conducted on a weekly basis.

4. <u>Disable any ports that are not in use</u>: Although this sounds like an obvious task that should be done, but very often, this goes overlooked. Many organizations leave their network ports wide open, thus leaving an extremely easy point of entry for the cyberattacker. It is

highly advised that your IT security staff should check for any open ports that are not being used on a weekly basis. If any are discovered, they should be closed off immediately. Of course, if there are any network ports that are open and being used, they must be secured as well, especially at the endpoints. This is critical for wireless devices, especially where Bluetooth is being used.

5. <u>Make use of multifactor authentication</u>: Many cybersecurity experts advocate the use of 2FA, but even this is not proving to provide adequate levels of security. Therefore, it is recommended that more than two layers of authentication should be implemented, especially at your endpoints. Perhaps consider implementing at least three to four layers of authentication, one of them which should be making use of biometric technology. This can guarantee much higher levels accuracy when confirming the identity of an individual.

6. <u>Implement the "Zero Trust Model" established by Forrester</u>: The traditional security models basically state the following:

The fundamental problem in network security is the broken trust model where cybersecurity pros, by default, trust the users and traffic inside their network, and assume that all those external to the network are untrusted.

(Source: 11.)

In other words, you can implicitly trust the objects and daily interactions ***within your IT infrastructure***, but ***not outside of it***. But with the Zero Trust Model, you there is absolutely ***no level of trust*** whatsoever, internal of external. Generally speaking, this can be implemented onto your endpoints with these five steps:

■ Identify and classify your sensitive information;

- Map the data flows that are coming to it and leaving it;
- Craft and implement your own unique Zero Trust Model to fit these particular data flows;
- Establish an automated rule-based system that will trigger the appropriate alerts and warnings;
- Keep monitoring the Zero Trust Model ecosystem on a daily basis.

7. <u>Make sure that your endpoints are well protected</u>: This means that you have implemented the right mixture of security technologies, primarily those of firewalls and routers. But the cardinal rule here is that ***<u>do not simply use the default settings that have been set up by the vendor</u>*** and assume that they will provide the adequate levels of security. These settings must be ***<u>set up and established that are dictated by specific security needs of your organization</u>***. Also keep in mind that many network infrastructures remain static in nature unless there is a specific reason to change them. Because of this, make sure that your VPN stays up to date and secure, especially when it comes to your employees accessing the endpoints through this.

8. <u>Make use of the Office 365 "Secure Score"</u>: Many businesses and corporations are now heavily dependent upon the tools and applications that reside within Office 365; and as a result, this has become a prime target for the cyberattacker. Microsoft provides a specialized tool called the "Secure Score", which is made available exclusively to the network administrator. With this, all of the Office 365 packages that are being used in your organization are closely scrutinized, such as the daily activities of your employees, and all of the relevant security settings. Once this task has been accomplished, you get a score (this is very similar to that of receiving a credit score). The higher it is, the more secure your Office 365 environment is, the lower it is, the less secure it is. All of

this means that you need to tweak and adjust the settings and configurations of the Office 365 portals that fit the security needs of your organization.

The Need for the SOAR Methodology

One thing that a CISO and his or her IT security team can do to get ready for a second onslaught off the novel COVID-19 virus is to make use of automation. This is where the roles of both AI and ML will come into play.

AI can be technically defined as follows:

> It is the science and engineering of making intelligent machines, especially intelligent computer programs. It is related to the similar task of using computers to understand human intelligence, but AI does not have to confine itself to methods that are biologically observable.
>
> *(Source: 12.)*

ML can be technically defined as follows:

> Machine learning is a branch of AI and computer science which focuses on the use of data and algorithms to imitate the way that humans learn, gradually improving its accuracy.
>
> *(Source: 13.)*

In this subsection of this chapter, we examine the SOAR methodology in more detail:

In today's business world, there is no doubt that the IT and network infrastructures of all sorts of businesses are starting to become complex, even if they have a cloud-based platform, such as that of Microsoft Azure. The need to centralize all monitoring of log events and the collection of mission-critical information and data is growing stronger day by day.

One such way to do this is to implement the SOAR methodology.

What Is SOAR All About?

It is an acronym that stands for security orchestration automation and response. It is a term that was actually developed by Gartner back in 2017. SOAR refers to the convergence of three types of cybersecurity technological platforms:

■ Security and automation;
■ Threat intelligence platforms;
■ Incident response tools.

What is unique about SOAR is that it is heavily reliant upon the principles of both AI and ML. Thus, the SOAR has been established to meet three primary objectives:

■ To automate the more routine and mundane processes of those tasks that are too time-consuming and laborious in nature by making use of various "Playbooks" (an example of this can be seen in Exhibit A);
■ To learn various pattern behaviors (such as that of threat vectors) that have occurred in the past, and try to model what future cyberattacks could potentially look like;
■ To filter out for false positives so that the IT security team is only presented with those alerts and warnings that are for real;
■ To create a unified view of all of the data and analytics that have been collected, as well as any pending cyber case management issues that are currently being worked on.

The bottom line is that the SOAR methodology has been created to protect a business entity form cyberattacks that originate from the external environment are trying to break into the lines of defense in order to reach the digital assets of a company which are internal.

A Deep Dive into SOAR

Now that the acronym has been defined, it is important to break down each of its individual components in further detail, which are as follows:

1. Security orchestration: Whenever there is a threat vector that is looming or even if a security breach has actually occurred, the IT security team is often tasked with the process having to interact with each and every security tool that has been deployed. Very often, the information and data that have been gathered and collected need to be reviewed manually, which, of course, can take a lot of time to accomplish. But through the orchestration of the resources, the processes, and the people that are needed to do all of this into a cohesive unit, the time to respond is significantly reduced.

2. Measurement: In this regard, the establishment of key metrics is a must so that those split-second decisions can be made at a moment's notice. Also, the flow of communication from the CIO/CISO to the IT security team (and vice versa) must also be established into a centralized environment. This where the role of a SIEM software package comes into play, such as that of Microsoft Sentinel. This aspect of SOAR (the "measurement") can be deployed into the SIEM, via the use of easy to see and understand dashboards that can be custom created.

3. Automation: When the IT security team is tasked to triage through the legitimate warnings and alerts that

they receive, this also has to be done on a manual basis. Although AI and ML are typically used to filter and weed out for the false positives (as previously mentioned), they can also be used to help automate and synchronize the triaging process on a 24 × 7 × 365 basis. This will allow the cyber analysts to quickly decide which ones are of the highest priority so that they can receive the quickest attention for resolution. AI and ML can also be used to centralize all of the warnings and messages that are coming from each and every network security tool that has been deployed by the business.

The Strategic Benefits of SOAR

Apart from unifying the various processes and task automation, SOAR brings other benefits as well, which are:

- It greatly improves the level of a company's cyber resiliency if that have been brought down by a security breach;
- It can aid in the investigation process, especially when it comes to forensics;
- Except for perhaps the SIEM, typically, no other hardware or software is needed to deploy the SOAR methodology. It is cross-compatible with many of the other security tools that are currently available today;
- It will keep your IT security team sharp, and on their A-Game at all times by only giving them the information/ data that are needed (separating the wheat from the chaff);
- It is primarily available as a hosted offering. This means that it is very affordable to use, and thus is highly

scalable as your security requirements and needs change in an ever-dynamic environment;
- It can make use of your existing security tools and technologies so that in the end, you will realize a much greater Return On Investment (ROI) on them.

The Need for the Use of the SIEM

One very valuable tool that has become recently available for the IT security team and his or her staff is that of the SIEM. Essentially, this is a unified dashboard in which all incoming threats, alerts, and warnings can be seen from just one dashboard. This will be of particular when the next large scale impact happens, whether it is manmade or natural.

In this subsection of this chapter, we do a deeper dive into it.

In dealing with today's cybersecurity threat landscape, businesses and corporations have deployed many tools from different vendors to beef up their lines of defense. The thinking here is that more is better, but this is only increasing the attack surface for the cyberattacker. There is now a fundamental shift in this kind of thinking, and CIOs and CISOs are starting to realize the importance of conducting security assessments to strategically place their tools.

But until this is fully realized, the IT security staffs at these organizations are continuously inundated with a lot of information and data that they must parse through. It can take hours if not days to filter through all of this.

What would be nice is to have a software package that can collect all this information and data and displace it into one central repository, using dashboards so that this can all be seen in one view. This is where the role of the SIEM comes into play.

The SIEM

Typically, this is the amount of information and data that an IT security team deals with daily, which is represented in the matrix below:

The Security Stack

Information Category	Collected Data
Money	Security Budget
Management	Security Policy
User	Security Awareness/Training and Detecting Any Erratic Behavior
Application	Software Configurations
Presentation	Server Operating System Configurations
Session (SSL)	Network Session Security
Transport (TCP/UDP)	Secure Port Binding; Port Security and Control
Network/Routing (IP/X)	Routing Protocol Control and Encryption
Data Link (Ethernet)	Local Area Network (LAN) and Wide Area Network (WAN) Security
Physical (Cable, Data Center Points of Entry)	Security and Access Control

(Source: 14.)

The SIEM (which stands for security information and event management) is an application that takes all the above and brings it down into one view (or even multiple views, depending upon the security requirements of the organization). Also, it can quickly capture any sort of abnormal or anomalous behavior in real time, and immediately notify the appropriate personnel about it. At its core, the SIEM can be thought of as a data aggregator that collects information from all the tools that are displaced at a business entity. This includes such as items as the network devices (such as the routers, firewalls, network intrusion devices, etc.), Servers, and the domain controllers. It also allows for the cybersecurity analyst to conduct forensic like research into security breaches that may have occurred.

How a SIEM Works

The diagram below illustrates the process as to how a SIEM works:

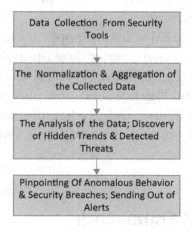

(*Source: 15*)

The Functionalities of a SIEM

A SIEM possesses the following functionalities:

1. Event and log data capture: The SIEM can be highly customizable in terms of the information and data that it collects, and only the most relevant pieces will be displayed. All of this is stored into one central repository, which allows for the business entity to come into compliance with regards to storage requirements.
2. Concise views: As described earlier, the SIEM presents a "birds' eye" view of what is transpiring. These views or dashboards can be custom created in order to meet the specific needs of the IT security staff.
3. Normalization: This involves two separate parts:
   - Breaking down all the techno jargon into a format that can be quickly and easily understood;
   - Mapping the data fields as established by the vendor to that of the end user (this is also referred to as "Field Mapping").
4. Correlation: Past trends can be matched up to new ones that have been discovered, thus providing a real sense of what is happening.
5. Scalability: A SIEM software application can be quickly ramped up or down, depending upon the changing needs of the organization. A typical example of this is when more intelligence feeds are plugged into the SIEM, so that it can "learn" and predict into the future.
6. Reporting: Continuous monitoring is available, 24 hours/ day x 7 days/week x 365 days/year.

The Zero Trust Framework

In order to fully make sure that their business will not become a victim of a cyberattack (such as phishing, domain heisting, spoofed websites, etc.), the CISO and his or her IT security team must make sure that each and every person is fully vetted before they can gain access to the shared network resources.

This is where the Zero Trust Framework will come into play, and is further reviewed in this subsection of this chapter.

Even despite the roles that password managers and 2FA play in preventing data hacks, these tools are simply not enough yet to prevent data hacks and breaches. What is needed is a very drastic approach, such as the Zero Trust Framework, in which absolutely no entity is trusted. This is the focal point of this article.

What Exactly Is Zero Trust?

In the traditional identity and access management (IAM) models, even though strong levels of authentication are more or less required, there is still an implicit level of trust that is often taken for granted. For example, the employees that have been around the longest in a business could bypass certain authentication mechanisms without being questioned at all.

But with the Zero Trust Framework, it takes this principle to yet another extreme in which nobody at all is trusted in both the internal and the external environments to your company. In other words, it is not just end users, but even devices, and the higher-ranking members of both the C-Suite and the board of directors cannot be trusted at all. In order to gain access to what is needed, all of these entities must be fully vetted and authenticated to the maximum level possible.

The use of multifactor authentication (MFA) is required, in which at least three layers (preferably even more) are used to order to 100% fully verify the device or the end user in question.

In fact, a key distinction with the Zero Trust Framework is that it is not typically used for just enhancing the primary lines of defense for the business. Rather, this new way of thinking in cybersecurity is further extended to protect **_each_ _and every_** server, workstation, and other assets that reside from within the IT infrastructure. This is also known as "Micro segmentation".

The Zero Trust Framework also consists of the following components:

- Policy enforcement and orchestration engines;
- High levels of encryption;
- Stronger levels of endpoint security;
- Role-based access control (RBAC);
- Logging and analytic tools.

How to Implement the Zero Trust Framework

Deploying this takes a lot of planning and should be done in a phased in approach. The following are key areas that you need to keep in mind as you deploy it:

1. Determine the interconnections: In today's environment, your digital assets are not just isolated to themselves. For example, your primary database will be connected with others, as well as to other servers, which are both physical and virtual in nature. Because of this, you also need to ascertain how these linkages work with another, and from there, determine the types of controls that can be implemented in between these digital assets so that they can be protected.

2. Understand and completely define what needs to be protected: With Zero Trust, you don't assume that your most vulnerable digital assets are at risk. Rather, you take

the position that everything is prone to a security breach, no matter how minimal it might be to your company. In this regard, you are taking a much more holistic view, in that you are not simply protecting what you think the different potential attack planes could be, but you are viewing this as an entire surface that needs 100% protection, on a 24 × 7 × 365 basis. So, you and your IT security team need to take a very careful inventory of everything digital that your company has, and from there, mapping out how each of them will be protected. So rather than having the mindset of one overall arching line of defense for your business, you are now taking the approach of creating many different "Micro Perimeters" for each individual asset.

3. <u>Crafting the Zero Trust Framework</u>: It is important to keep in mind instituting this does not take a "One Size Fits All" approach. Meaning, what may work for one company will not work for your business. The primary reason for this is that not only do you have your own unique set of security requirements, but the protection surface and the linkages that you have determined will be unique to you as well. Therefore, you need to take the mindset that you need to create your framework as to what your needs are at that moment in time, as well as considering projected future needs.

4. <u>Implement how the Zero Trust Framework will be determined</u>: The final goal to be achieved is how it will be monitored on a real-time basis. In this particular instance, you will want to make use of what is known as a SIEM software package. This is an easy to deploy tool that will collect all of the logging and activity information, as well as all of the warnings and alerts and put them into one central view. The main advantage of this is that your IT security team will be able to triage and act upon those threat variants almost instantaneously.

The Advantages

These are as follows:

1. <u>A much greater level of accountability</u>: When the remote workforce started to take full swing last year because of COVID-19, many companies were in a rush to issue company devices. Unfortunately, not every business entity could do this, and as a result, employees were forced to use their own devices in order to conduct their daily tasks associated with work. Unfortunately, this also triggered a whole new host of security issues. Thankfully, as organizations are starting to implement the concept of Zero Trust, there is now a much higher degree of accountability with devices being used for this regard. For example, if an employee wishes to gain access to corporate resources on their own device, they can no longer do so. They now must use company-issued equipment which possesses these authentication mechanisms so that access can be granted.

2. <u>It facilitates the use of centralized monitoring</u>: When security tools and technologies are used in different combinations with no planning in mind, it can be very difficult for the IT security team to keep track of all of the warnings and alerts that are coming in. This can make it very difficult to triage and escalate the real cyber threats that are out there. But with the Zero Trust methodology, since each device is accounted for in a logical manner, a centralized approach can now be utilized. One typical example of this is what is known as the security incident and event management software application. With this, not only can the false positives be filtered out by making use of both AI and ML, but the legitimate warnings and alerts can be presented in a real-time basis through a centralized dashboard. Thus, this allows the IT security team to be far more proactive, and in turn,

greatly reduce the response times to combating various threat vectors.

3. <u>An almost total elimination of passwords</u>: The password has long been the de facto standard in order to authenticate an individual to gain access to shared resources. But even despite the advancements of password managers, people are still stuck in their old ways, making passwords even more vulnerable than they were before. With the Zero Trust Framework, much greater efforts are now taken to totally eradicate the use of passwords and use much more robust authentication tools. For example, there is now a heavy reliance upon using biometric technology. With this, a unique physiological or behavioral trait is extracted from the individual in order to 100% confirm their identity, which obviously, nobody else possesses. The biggest advantage of this is that different kinds and types of biometric modalities (such as fingerprint recognition, iris recognition, facial recognition, etc.) can be implemented at different points in the corresponding security layers. For example, they can be used individually, and in tandem with each other to create a very secure environment.

4. <u>Scalability is offered</u>: With the remote workforce now guaranteed to be a long-term phenomenon, many companies are now opting to make greater usage of cloud-based resources, such as those offered by the AWS or Microsoft Azure. There are of course those entities that still choose to have a brick-and-mortar presence, and to a certain degree, still have some remnants of an on-premises solution. But whatever option is chosen, the Zero Trust Framework allows the seamless transfer for apps, digital assets, and even the confidential information and data (especially the PII datasets) from one place to another in a much more secure fashion.

5. Breaking in becomes close to impossible: Before the COVID-19 pandemic hit, many businesses adopted what is known as the "Perimeter Security" approach to protecting their digital assets. This simply means that there was only one line of defense separating the internal environment from the external environment. As a result, if the cyberattacker were to penetrate through this, they could gain access to just about anything in the IT and network infrastructure and move covertly in a lateral fashion. But with the Zero Trust Framework, the implementation of multiple layers of security means that it becomes that much harder for the cyberattacker to gain access to the proverbial "Crown Jewels", as it will take much longer to break through every line of defense, as they try to go deeper in. In the end, more than likely, he or she will just give up.

6. Greater adherence to compliance: With the heightened enforcement of the GDPR, CCPA, HIPAA, etc., companies now must come into compliance with all of the various statutes and provisions that are applicable to them. By adopting the Zero Trust Framework, businesses will now be assured of keeping up that level of compliance, as they will be forced now to implement the right set of controls (which are essentially the authentication mechanisms) in order to protect their PII datasets, which is what is being scrutinized the most by auditors and regulators.

References

1. https://www.varonis.com/blog/incident-response-plan/
2. https://smallbiztrends.com/2017/04/not-prepared-for-data-loss.html
3. https://www.gartner.com/it-glossary/bia-business-impact-analysis

4. https://blog.icorps.com/it-disaster-recovery-facts
5. https://www.senseofsecurity.com.au/consulting/red-team-testing/
6. https://www.swordshield.com/security-assessments/purple-team-assessment-service/
7. https://www.techradar.com/news/what-is-a-dark-web-scan-and-do-you-need-one
8. https://www.raytheon.com/sites/default/files/cyber/rtnwcm/groups/iis/documents/content/proactive-hunting-datasheet.pdf
9. https://www.darkreading.com/partner-perspectives/juniper/proactive-threat-hunting-taking-the-fight-to-the-enemy-/a/d-id/1331084
10. https://go.crowdstrike.com/rs/281-OBQ-266/images/WhitepaperProactiveHunting.pdf
11. https://www.insight.com/en_US/learn/content/2017/09132017-6-best-practices-for-complete-network-and-endpoint-security.html
12. https://www.ibm.com/cloud/learn/what-is-artificial-intelligence
13. https://www.ibm.com/cloud/learn/machine-learning
14. https://www.tripwire.com/state-of-security/incident-detection/log-management-siem/what-is-a-siem/
15. https://www.varonis.com/blog/what-is-siem/

Chapter 4

Conclusions

Overall, this book has been designed to be a "Guide" for the CISO, or for that matter, anybody else in the IT security team holding the title of Manager or higher. True, the world has seen many rough periods, but what makes the novel COVID-19 virus so unprecedented is that it was first thought it would be contained from within the confines of China.

But what the world did not realize is how quickly that it would spread. It all started back in December 2020, and then it really proliferated back in January 2021. As it was stated in Chapter 1 of this book, it spread around the world like wildfire. It literally rattled both financial markets and every industry imaginable.

The bottom line is that this virus is not going to disappear soon. Unfortunately, it is going to be with mankind for a long period of time. It has been forecasted that there will be many variants of this, and we are only seeing the surface of it. The first variant is called the "Delta Variant". Many health experts expect that there will be more variants, such as:

- The Gamma Variant;
- The Lambda Variant;
- The Alpha Variant.

DOI: 10.1201/9781003279143-4

Even people who have been vaccinated are still getting this virus. Many health experts fear that it could take years until the novel COVID-19 virus has completely "calmed down", in many ways like the influenza virus. At least with this, even with the new strains that emerge, vaccines can be developed very quickly, based upon statistical modeling that takes place.

Aside from the financial and individual human impacts that the novel COVID-19 virus has made upon the world, one of its largest impacts has been upon Corporate America, as well as other businesses worldwide. For example, the chapter provides more details what the lessons have been learned in terms of the novel COVID-19 virus in the last year and a half.

But believe it or not, there is some benefit that has come out of the novel COVID-19 virus. For example, the concept of a near 99% remote workforce was thought to happen in about four to five years from now. But it happened in a time period of just three months. True, many mistakes were made from the standpoint of cybersecurity, such as hastily deploying devices without all of the security protocols on them and letting employees use their own devices called "Bring Your Own Device" or "BYOD" in short.

Then there was the intermingling of the home and corporate networks, which made more of a nightmare for the IT security team as they had an extremely hard time trying to deploy the needed software patches and upgrades in a timely manner. Of course, who could also forget about "Zoombombing"?

That was a cyberattack in which the cyberattacker could literally break through a private conference, and hijack it, and steal any confidential information and data, and sell on the dark web, for a rather nice profit. Then there were also those cyberattacks that involved the heisting of domain names, and from there, create phony and fictitious websites.

It should be noted that not only financial and banking websites were hit, but many medical-based websites were also impacted, even those that were just simply providing information, such as that of the World Health Organization, also known as the "WHO". As vaccines started to roll out from Pfizer, Moderna, and Johnson and Johnson, many other fake websites came up as well, which offered fake vaccines as well as fake vaccination cards.

The novel COVID-19 virus has also led to other controversial topics, such as having a novel COVID-19 virus passport. The basic concept of this is that this would be a proof that an individual has been vaccinated as he or she travels to other countries abroad. But many privacy rights groups have labeled this as being too discriminatory like the biometric passport, in which an individual is identified by their unique physiological and/or behavioral traits.

One of the controversial topics that still remains is really where did the novel COVID-19 virus originate? There are two main theories behind this:

■ It originated from the meat markets in the Wuhan of China;
■ An individual literally ate a bat, and this caused the novel COVID-19 virus to spread from an animal host to the human host;
■ It came out of a lab experiment that literally went bad.

Recently, the Biden Administration launched a study on this, but the evidence that was presented in the findings was deemed to be too inconclusive. But nonetheless, it is expected that this kind of investigation will still continue in the long term.

One of the other "good" things that have happened as a result of the novel COVID-19 virus is the use of cloud-based platforms, such as Amazon Web Services (AWS) and Microsoft Azure. With this, many on-premises solutions can now be moved here, and thus, the remote workforce can now access all of the shared resources that they need quickly and easily from any device that they choose from anywhere and anytime in the world.

Overall, this book has examined the following topics:

■ The molecular biology of the novel COVID-19 virus;
■ The lessons that have been learned from it;
■ How the CISO and their IT security team can apply the lessons learned by using the right toolsets and methodologies.

Hopefully, with the insights that have been presented in this book, the CISO and their IT security team will be able to handle another disaster like the novel COVID-19 virus or even if it is a man-made disaster.

But here is betting the odds that it may never happen.

Index

Page numbers in *italics* refer to figures and page numbers in **bold** refer to tables